Fantasy Map Making

A step-by-step guide for worldbuilders

Jesper Schmidt

Copyright © 2018 Jesper Schmidt

Published 2018 by Jesper Schmidt

Book design by Autumn Raven

Copyright © 2018 Jesper Schmidt

No part of this book may be reproduced in any manner without written permission, except in the case of brief quotations included in critical articles and reviews. For information, please contact the author via www.jesperschmidt.com.

Published by Fantasy Publishing

A STEP-BY-STEP GUIDE FOR WORLDBUILDERS

For your benefit I have created a free worksheet that goes along with this book. You can *download it from here*: https://www.jesperschmidt.com/fantasy-map-making-download/.

I recommend that you print a copy – it's only 11 pages – and use it as a checklist. The added benefit is that it includes some inspirational questions that can come in handy as a supplement.

Note: If you are reading this book in paperback format, simply type the above link into your browser and it will take you directly to the download page.

IS THIS BOOK FOR ME?

If you are reading this with the intention of creating a map of an imaginary world, being a fantasy novel, a movie, a video game or a role-playing game, then **Fantasy Map Making** is written for your benefit.

It's a type of *checklist-compendium* that takes you through the entire map creation process, step by step. Most creative people – and I will assume that you are one, too – will have a wealth of inventive ideas for their fantasy settings. However, without the knowledge of geography and climate to match them, they end up creating a non-realistic version that will break immersion.

That word, *immersion*, is an extremely important one in the context of map making.

It's your job as the creator of the fantastical realm to forge a universe which offers infinite possibilities, yet is kept easy to interpret and understand. Your audience might not be able to put their finger on it, but most will intuitively know that something is off if a map doesn't depict reality correctly.

For this reason, I'm going to talk a lot about realism when it comes to creating your map.

I do respect the fact that many fantasy worlds are often shown as medieval Europe, without Christianity and magic added, but even so, this is still where I will ground us. You see, **Fantasy Map Making** will assume that you are redrawing an Earth-like setting.

A STEP-BY-STEP GUIDE FOR WORLDBUILDERS

Most fantasy makers are headed in this direction anyway, and for good reason. I just mentioned it: *immersion*. So, unless you are en route to a completely alien planet, the teachings of this book will be for you.

That said, feel free to ignore the guidelines as they are written. It's your art, after all… And if you want to, you can always blame magic. Besides, knowing how things generally go in the real world gives you the power to judge what to change in order to craft extraordinaries and fantasy.

The strength of this guidebook is that it will show you exactly how to translate your ideas into a realistic-looking map. On the flip side, this is also its greatest weakness.

Fantasy Map Making is *not* a publication on worldbuilding.

Although, I will touch slightly on nation-building – almost solely in relation to placing them on your fantasy map – you won't find information on how to develop a fantasy world here. If that is your aim, then this is *not* the book you are looking for.

Since I write fantasy fiction, this is also the angle I'm coming from, but know that when I use the word *audience*, don't read it as only pertaining to readers of fiction, but also someone watching a movie, playing a video game, or participating in a role-playing game. The contents of this book are applicable for everyone interested in creating fantasy maps.

> **Fantasy Map Making** is a full guide, created specifically to assist you in crafting a realistic, Earth-like fantasy map.

Inside these pages are also a number of pictures. They are placed with the intention of supplying you with visual aids in the creation process. With that said, ***please note*** that the eBook version of **Fantasy Map Making** has been professionally formatted with the best of intentions to avoid oddly displayed pictures across different types of e-readers. If your particular device just happens to be the exception, I hope you will be forgiving. I have done my best to prevent that from happening.

SECOND EDITION CHANGES

One of the things I needed when I began to write my first fantasy trilogy, back in 2015, was a map of my new fantasy setting, *Erisdün*.

I created my first fantasy world about 30 years ago and ever since, as a child, I first became acquainted with the *Dragonlance Chronicles* by Margaret Weis and Tracy Hickman, together with the role-playing game *Dungeons & Dragons*, fantasy has been a huge passion for me.

Deep down in my heart, I believe that a true fantasy novel, board game or role-playing game – take your pick – isn't complete without a map, so it goes without saying that this was the first item on my to-do list.

You see, I'm very much a *checklist type* of a person. The structure of this book will prove as much.

Delving into the creating of fantasy books – not only for my own pleasure, but also with the intention of selling them – I found it important to create a map that would do the novels justice. I browsed through the Amazon Kindle store in search of eBooks to assist me in this undertaking. I was going to do it right this time. My home-made slapstick approach was not going to cut it for a commercial product like a fantasy trilogy.

I found plenty of books on *how to draw a map*, but none about *how to design one*. I wanted to know how to create a realistic map, so I researched how in depth.

As a result, **Fantasy Map Making** became the first book I ever wrote, and as some Amazon reviewers have rightly pointed out, the first edition, released on the 1st of August 2016, had some weak spots. Writing a book is much harder than it seems, but now that I have a few under my belt, I took the feedback on-board. I reinvested a lot of time, energy and money to do the content of this resource guide full justice and make it the best it can be. It deserved no less.

My hope is that the steps I have laid out in the pages to come will help you in all your endeavors to create amazing maps for your future worlds.

It's equally daunting and exciting to create a setting that will truly *immerse* your audience – being readers or role-playing gamers – and having to reinvent the wheel over and over, researching the same topic multiple times, won't make it any easier. I now give you a resource guide which has been designed for the sole purpose of carrying you through the entire process step by step.

Welcome to the new, second edition of **Fantasy Map Making**.

მა

This book is structured in parts and should be read in order the first time around. Later, you can dip into the chapters that are most relevant to your map making task of the day.

Below is a list of the most significant updates to the *second edition*.

The rest of the chapters have also been re-edited, most of them also updated with fresh content.

Every single word of this book has been revisited.

Is This Book For Me? & The Amazing World of Maps

I added both these chapters to the beginning of the book – neither existed in the first edition – to allow readers a better understanding of this book's premise and, at the same time, include more context around the use of maps in the real world, flavored with some personal stories.

What is a Fantasy Map?

Compared to the original version, this chapter is almost in its entirety rewritten. It's considerably expanded, without dragging on, and provides a much better answer to the question asked than the first edition ever did.

Excuses

While the five excuses are the same as the ones listed in the first edition of fantasy map making, I decided to frame them in a different and more guiding tone.

Software

The list of possible software solutions for the purpose of map making has been doubled compared to what was listed in the first edition. That way, you have more to choose from.

My Recommendation

I rewrote parts of this chapter and was pleased to be able to add an example of what a high-end, fully hand-drawn map looks like. Enjoy.

Steps Five and Six

Both these sections have almost been rewritten in entirety. An instructional map has also been added to carry you through the remaining parts of the book to illustrate each step of the process. This will function as an improved learning experience as you get to see the creation of a map while you create your own.

Steps Seven through Thirteen

The basics of Step Seven are similar to the first edition of *Fantasy Map Making*, but more details have been added to make it a more fulfilling step in the process.

Step Fourteen

This is a completely new step to the fantasy map making process which was never mentioned in the first edition.

A STEP-BY-STEP GUIDE FOR WORLDBUILDERS

THE AMAZING WORLD OF MAPS

Cast your mind back, for a moment, to the 20th-century competition between the two Cold War rivals, the Soviet Union and the United States, for supremacy in space flight capabilities. Before the Space Race began, no human being had ever seen our home planet, Earth, from high above. Today, we take orbital images for granted, but at that time, not that long ago, no one had ever seen the globe from a viewpoint of a large map.

The fact that we view the nearby and the faraway in the same frame is perhaps why mankind has fallen so in love with maps with such a strange intensity. Well, at least a fraction of us have – you and me included – and it seems to me that this appetite is often rooted in childhood. It's a well-known fact that very young children can understand maps with no training whatsoever. Scientists have speculated that there is some kind of innate ability that makes people, regardless of culture, able to interpret maps. New research has shown that this isn't true for everyone, but it only proves the point I was making earlier: the one about *immersion*.

> *If you create a fantasy map that isn't true to the laws of nature, you will be running the risk that your audience will be able to tell.*

Maps are in fact older that the art of writing, and one might say that they are almost too convenient when it comes to understanding place. In their simplest interpretation, all maps show two things: places where you have already been, and places yet to visit. They are indeed wonderful tools that help our mind to separate things; the land of the good guys vs. that of the bad guys; the safe place vs. the unsafe one; the known vs. the unknown.

In their early versions maps did share some similarities with modern cartography, but their primary significance at the time was probably more related to spirituality. Over millennia they evolved into what we recognize as a map today. The first cardinal directions were first seen on Babylonian clay tablet maps from five thousand years ago. The cardinal directions are the arrows on the compass rose, yet the first true compass rose didn't appear until the year 1375 in the Catalan Atlas.

Another well known map key, the scale, wasn't seen on maps until three thousand years after the Babylonian clay tablet maps. The oldest found was on a bronze plate from China's Zhou dynasty.

To find the oldest surviving version of a paper map, we need to fast-forward several centuries and into the time of Christ. Here a Greek papyrus illustrated the Iberian Peninsula.

We map-lovers have always been fascinated by such portrayals. Bartolomé de Las Casas, a biographer of Christopher Columbus, wrote that the explorer's first Atlantic voyage was inspired by nautical charts received from the Italian mathematician Paolo Toscanelli.

Las Casas wrote: "He did not doubt he should find those lands that were marked upon it."

In all fairness, historians believe that Viking sailors landed in what is now known as Canada around AD 1000. This was 500 years before the birth of Christopher Columbus, but it doesn't change the fact that a map changed the course of history when Columbus *did* arrive in America in the year of 1492.

While the evolution of map making might have been a slow and gradual process, it's still as if our map-loving minds are rewired for eternity when, as children, we first discover maps. It turns into an irresistible passion that never leaves us. Or at least it did for me.

I clearly recall an A3-sized piece of paper that my younger brother and I spread out across our parents' dinner table. It was one of those brown, recycled pieces of copy paper. On it we drew random caves, cities, mountains, forests, and of course… monster lairs. This became our fantasy world and we laid siege on that dinner table for the entire weekend. I'm sure my parents were much less delighted, but to us it added a completely new layer of depth to our play.

I must have been around ten years old at the time, which puts us back more than twenty-five years, so, to be honest, I cannot be entirely sure that this was indeed our first map, but I know for a fact that I have loved maps ever since. There was no going back. From here on forward, hand-scribbled maps were added to more and more of our games – this was before iPads, tablets and real computer games.

When we played with our race cars, maps were created to show the circuits on which we raced. Our game of Cowboys and Indians also included a mapped-out terrain in which we conducted our battles. Even with Lego, we laid out the landscape before we let combat commence.

For some reason, we always ended up coming back to fantasy, though. Perhaps it was how maps suggest there to be an adventure waiting beyond the mountains, but it always fascinated my young mind.

One day, my grandfather took me to his desk and placed me on his lap. He would usually spend the afternoons sitting in his swivel chair doing crossword puzzles, yet on that day he showed me a brand new decorative desktop globe. It even had a light bulb that would illuminate the Earth from the inside. I was completely mesmerized.

I sat there for hours, spinning it, exploring all the different regions and countries of the world. The mountain ranges had a special kind of allure for me, and each time my eye caught sight of one, I traced my fingers across it.

Then there were all those amazing place names. Brazilian rivers ("Acaraú River…Ribeirão Crisóstomo…Umbuzeiro River…") and the mountains of India ("Aq Tash… Kirat Chuli… Satopanth…"). They all seemed secret phrases. If only I whispered them loud enough, I could enter a magical realm.

Given how exploration of new worlds lies at the core of the fantasy genre, it's hardly surprising that maps became such a trusted companion on my imaginary journeys.

I am, to this day, mystified by the fact that maps meant so much to me – and to a large extent, still do. In practical terms, maps are just a way of organizing information, but nevertheless, I distinctly remember how the maps J.R.R. Tolkien included in *The Lord of the Rings* were able to deepen my sense of *immersion* into the presented world of *Middle-Earth*.

All I can say is I believe there is something innate about maps that charms us: this easy and simple way of picturing our world. If there is a map on the wall, it just won't leave me alone.

If I close my eyes, and stay completely still, I can almost hear it calling.

CONTENTS

Fantasy Maps — 1
   What Is A Fantasy Map? — 2
   Are Maps Even Important — 5
   Excuses — 7
      Excuse #1 — 9
      Excuse #2 — 10
      Excuse #3 — 11
      Excuse #4 — 12
      Excuse #5 — 13
      So, Do You Need A Map? — 17
Step One: Something to Consider — 19
   Think, Then Act — 20
      The Wish List — 24
      A Mental Note — 26
Step Two: Tools — 29
   Your Tool Of Choice — 30
      Hand Drawn — 31
      Software — 37
      Hire A Professional — 42

A STEP-BY-STEP GUIDE FOR WORLDBUILDERS

My Recommendation	45
Step Three: The Overview	51
Designing Your Map	52
Step Four: Make A Sketch	53
The Size Of Your World	54
Walking	57
On Horseback	58
On Wheels	59
By Boat	60
And There Was Magic	61
Finishing the Sketch	62
Step Five: Let There Be Land	65
Tectonic Plates	66
What Are Tectonic Plates	67
Adding Tectonic Plates To Your Map	71
Step Six: Terraforming	75
What Are Climate Zones	76
Adding Clmate Zones To The Map	79
Weather Patterns	84
Mountains And Deserts	87
Step Seven: Islands and Lakes	93
Islands	94
Lakes	95
Step Eight: Rivers	99
Rivers And How To Place Them	100
Step Nine: Forest	105
And There Were Trees	106
Step Ten: Countries	109
Nation-Building	110
Countries And Borders	112
Settlements	114

A STEP-BY-STEP GUIDE FOR WORLDBUILDERS

Step Eleven: Roads	117
Arteries Of A Nation	118
Step Twelve: Fantasy	121
Wait… Where Is The Fantasy	122
Step Thirteen: Final Touches	125
The Map Key	126
Due Diligence	128
Step Fourteen: Map Master	131
Documenting The Realm	132
Appendices	137
Appendix A: List of Tools	138
Appendix B: Terrain Sub-Types	139

FANTASY MAPS

WHAT IS A FANTASY MAP?

We all know that a map constitutes a landscape drawn on a piece of paper – electronically or by hand. We also know that it's a symbolized representation of a geographical reality, representing a number of selected features or characteristics, and is by design intended to show us spatial relationships.

However, we only need to go back five or six hundred years to find that there was no clear distinction between fantasy maps and what we today would classify as "real" maps. In fact, back then, maps often had fantastic places included on them. For instance, from the Book of Revelation, the lands of Gog and Magog were situated by the Caspian Sea, with a wall that Alexander the Great had supposedly built around it. You could find Noah's ark in Turkey, and a ring of fire surrounding Paradise in the east.

With the rise of science fiction and fantasy writing, later accompanied by television and video games, fantasy maps increased not only in number, but also in imagination. They became places of *immersive* escapism.

As the bestselling fantasy writer Brandon Sanderson says, "The hallmark of epic fantasy is *immersion*. That's why I've always included maps in my books. I believe the map prepares your mind to experience the wonder."

Brandon Sanderson was the guy who was handpicked by the author Robert Jordan's widow to complete the world-renowned *Wheel of Time* series. Brandon Sanderson's novel, *The Way of Kings*, included no less than nine maps when it was published.

Yet, he is far from the only one with a fascination for maps. Places like Hogwarts from *Harry Potter* have been mapped out in the greatest of details, and most fantasy computer games rely heavy on maps, too. Not to mention probably one of the most famous fantasy maps of all time – the *Hundred Acre Wood* by E.H. Shepard which first appeared in 1926 as part of the *Winnie the Pooh* children's stories.

This might easily have been the first map many children of the time had ever seen, and perhaps many grew so fond of it because it clearly imitates the style of a child. It has misspellings and the incorporated touch of humor, in that the four points of the compass rose spell out P-O-O-H, brings a certain charm that is hard to resist.

As mentioned previously, I believe many of us find a love for maps during childhood. I never found myself fully *immersed* in C.S. Lewis's story about *The Lion, the Witch and the Wardrobe*, though. The forest of Narnia was just depicted as a cluster of trees, whereas Tolkien created elaborate landscapes in comparison.

Fantastic maps didn't really catch on until Tolkien's time: that is less than a century ago. In fact, if you think about it, most maps on the market are a fairly recent development, with almost none of them being more than five hundred years old. Yet, old maps have an allure to them. They come with a certain aura of mysticism.

So, in our attempt to define what a fantasy map truly is, let's once again travel to *Middle-Earth*. This is a place that I absolutely adore, so there will be several references to it in the pages to come.

When J.R.R. Tolkien published *The Hobbit* in 1937, followed by *The Lord of the Rings* trilogy in the 1950s, he also gave birth to the epic fantasy genre as we know it today. In his books we found maps that were imaginary in content, yet retained traces from the "real" world. The geography was to a large extent based on Europe and to support a prehistorical illusion he had it hand-drawn in ink with pictorial detail. It's not in the slightest far-fetched to claim that Tolkien made maps an integral part of fantasy worlds as we know them today – be it in fiction, video games or role-playing games.

Audiences who love fantasy don't mind being dropped into the deep end. They love studying the odd names and wonder about the arcane histories. Isn't it so that maps just tell a different kind of story than words ever will? When our eyes are free to wander, we are able to take the geography in all at once. We can let ourselves get absorbed by the exotic details.

All places, even those of the "real" world have an element of fantasy about them when shown on a map. Yet, even when fantasy maps look medieval, they have almost nothing in common. True medieval maps were pretty useless to people of the time. Those maps often listed locations linearly, and on occasions used the Roman scholar Ptolemy's grid of latitude and longitude. That is not how fantasy maps are built.

In truth, modern fantasy maps probably owe quite a lot to children's books. I have mentioned a few already, but even *The Hobbit* was originally intended as a children's book.

An overwhelming majority of fantasy maps are not representations of geographical reality. They are fictional maps and need not be a representation of Earth as we know it. Yet, they still need to toe a line between the imaginary world, and that of our modern mind which is trained to interpret GPS and Google Maps.

We have come full circle and now need, once more, to mention the word with which we began: *immersion.*

If your mountains are placed oddly, you have rivers splitting instead of combining, or country borders placed nowhere near natural barriers, then you better have a really good explanation for it, because your audience will be able to tell.

When creating fantasy maps, I find it my job, as the creator, to maintain *immersion* by portraying the imaginary world in a way that, for the most part, is grounded in reality as we know it. To me a fantasy map is one that enhances the ability to captivate the audience's mind and let them accept the parts that are truly fantastic as nothing out of the ordinary.

To achieve just that, the teachings of this book will keep us rooted in familiar elements and let things develop from a mold of reality.

ARE MAPS EVEN IMPORTANT?

By now, I probably don't need to explain how I believe any good fantasy world deserves a map. However, there are those fantasy authors and creators who would disagree with me.

So, in order to explore whether or not maps are important, let me begin by playing devil's advocate for a moment. Why is it that some creators find maps unimportant?

Some view the maps as nothing but a cliche. A trope of fantasy, arising only because J.R.R. Tolkien used one. Terry Goodkind (#1 *New York Times* bestselling author) once said that he considered maps a distraction from the story. Others agree with him. There are even readers who insist that maps can be "a bit silly".

A few claims that a map is a spoiler – arguing that when the map shows three major locations in the world, lo and behold, the characters end up going there.

I won't argue against the fact that some maps can be bizarre and goofy, but when done right, they are anything but. It's not entirely true that all maps can be viewed as spoilers either. Take the *Kingkiller Chronicle* by Patrick Rothfuss as an example: some very important places aren't even marked on the map.

Opinions are all well and good, but I much prefer quantitative data if I can get my hands on it. Fantasy map making is a very niche subject matter, though, so in search of answers, my best option was to go on a long Google rampage. I wanted to know how common fantasy maps really are in works of fiction.

While I did uncover all sorts of material – and it all comes with a sprinkle of unscientific salt – this is my condensed and short bullet-point conclusion:

I. 33% of fantasy novels contain a map;
II. Maps are more common for novels set in a secondary world, i.e. not historical fantasy set on Earth;
III. 75% of novels that do feature a map only contain a single map.

A well-known exception to the third point is J.R.R. Tolkien's *The Lord of the Rings*. It holds a large-scale map of the Shire, a smaller one for the entire western part of *Middle-Earth,* and a medium scale map of *Gondor* and *Mordor.*

With only 33% of fantasy novels containing a map, one must think that maps are not the obligatory necessity they are widely held to be.

However, maps not only help to understand where things are located, they not only help getting a grasp of distance, they not only increase the sense of wonder, but they also help to deepen *immersion.* That is alpha omega and why I believe that maps are hugely important.

EXCUSES

If maps are truly so important, how can it be that most fantasy novelists aren't adding maps to their books? Why is it that some game developers and role-players decide to proceed without completing the world they labored so hard over with a map?

As data just showed us, 33% of fantasy novels contain a map, yet I cannot believe that this percentage also means that only a third of us fantasy creators find maps important. There must be something else at play here. Something that apparently makes many shy away from including maps in their fantasy works.

So, for those out there who want to create maps, but have decided not to, the topic of excuses has to be addressed.

In the context of map making, excuses are rationalizations which we make to ourselves, as invented reasoning, to prevent us from achieving the task at hand. Psychologists place it in the self-handicapping category, but it stems from a deeper, unconscious desire to protect ourselves against anxiety and shame.

Some people will have concerns over doing something wrong, or having their map judged by others. If this is the reason why we aren't seeing more maps in fantasy, then it's also very likely that the fourteen steps, as laid out in this book, never will get actioned by more than the aforementioned 33% of us.

Fear is a feeling that we need to eliminate all traces of. It traps and locks us away within our comfort zone. The good news it that such feelings, in part, develop as a result of a lack of information. From that perspective, the guidance offered by this book is intended to bridge such a gap.

Lacking knowledge about map making will naturally lead to loss of confidence, which consequently will be the reason for not creating a map and instead make excuses to artificially inflate one's self-esteem. As long as we don't challenge ourselves and take on the task of cartography, we are taking no risks, and with no risks we feel safe.

All we are really doing in this state, though, is creating an illusion of security. The fear is still there, and it will continue to persist until we stop trying to mask it with painkillers, and instead decide to overcome it. The more anxious we feel about map making, the more likely we are to build barriers that shift the focus to the excuses that impede our chances of success.

Making changes in our behavior is often the most difficult part. The first step is admitting to ourselves that we are making excuses in the first place, but it's absolutely imperative that we challenge ourselves if we are to reach new heights.

I would love to see more fantasy maps in the world, so here are five excuses that you might be making:

EXCUSE #1

"I can't draw."

Fortunately, you don't have to be an artist to create a fantasy map.

It doesn't really matter if it looks like a three-year-old drew it, or if you feel as if you're unable to make it look any good.

If your creation is purely for your own benefit, to give you a better idea of what your world looks like – which in itself might be the most important thing – then borrowing a piece of crayon from the kids' room and drawing a rudimentary map is more than sufficient.

On the other hand, if you intend the map to be included in a published work, or you want something that looks professional for your gaming group, then fear not. I promise that I will cover how to achieve just that in *Step Two*.

Don't let the fact that you can't draw hold you back. I can't either, so let's grab a pencil together.

EXCUSE #2

"The world is too large or too small!"

Well... if several maps are good enough for the likes of J.R.R. Tolkien and Brandon Sanderson, then they can be for your world, too.

Your big world, with multiple continents, can fit on separate maps, or you could cut back on the details and create a map that only shows the main features of your world in its entirety.

If your world is too small, then mapping it out should also be that much simpler. You can pour in those details that we just excluded from the world-spanning map and explore the smaller areas more fully. Make them truly rich for your audience.

At the root of this excuse might be the fact that you need to do a bit of planning beforehand. If that is what paralyzes you with fear, then we will soon get further into this as we reach *Step One*.

EXCUSE #3

"The novel is too long or not good enough for a map!"

This one is primarily an excuse used by novelists, and I hate to think how readers are cheated out of a map to guide them through imaginary places. A piece of fiction can never be too long to negate the importance of giving the audience a visual aid to help them enjoy the story laid out in front of them.

The fear at play here is likely one of the following: motivation, creativity (we will come back to this one with excuse #5), patience, or persistence.

All of these qualities are essential if we are going to make things work. Not only for map creation, but also for everything of value that you want to create in life.

No matter what, we have to combat this one.

EXCUSE #4

"I do not have the time or energy!"

All creation is difficult and establishing a captivating fantasy setting might just be one of the most difficult ones.

At the heart of this excuse lies a lack of passion, focus, discipline and direction.

It could suggest that priorities are out of sorts and there may be a lack of ability to manage time effectively, but it might also be an unwillingness to take the time needed to do the necessary and get a map created. In fact, the causes for this excuse can very often be narrowed down to procrastination or laziness.

Please don't cut yourself short. You owe more to yourself, your audience, and the hard labor you have poured into your creation.

Now, go crown it with a map.

EXCUSE #5

"I have no inspiration!"

Another way of expressing this is: *"I'm not creative enough."* If one considers our typical routines and the rituals we partake in throughout the day, we most often find that inspiration isn't a problem.

Digging a little deeper often leads to the fact that a lack of inspiration is most often caused by many interrelated factors that at first seem unrelated. For instance, a lack of sleep could be causing you to feel tired and thus lead to a lack of inspiration. Perhaps it's the diet that causes sleepless nights, or the lack of sleep is a result of not getting enough exercise throughout the week. Moreover, this could be caused by working too long hours which prevents allocating time for exercising.

Whatever it is, the more patterns we find, the more likely it is that we are able to identify where the lack of inspiration stems from.

That said, the issue might be much more mundane than that. Perhaps an Internet search for fantasy maps is really all that is needed to let inspiration find you. Don't feel guilty about this in the slightest. There is nothing wrong with getting the creative juices flowing by being influenced by others.

Take George R. R. Martin as an example. In an interview at the Edinburgh International Book Festival he mentioned how Tolkien had been a huge influence on his work, "I revere *The Lord of the Rings*, I reread it every few years, it had an enormous effect on me as a kid. In some sense, when I started this saga [author's note: he is referring to the *A Song of Ice and Fire* series] I was replying to Tolkien, but even more to his modern imitators… I wanted to combine the wonder and image of Tolkien fantasy with the gloom of historical fiction."

George R. R. Martin is saying that he wanted to create a rich fictional setting where readers could lose themselves, just as he had reading *The Lord of the Rings* as a child. Once again, we see how a love for fantasy is found at a young age, and while the themes in *A Song of Ice and Fire* are different from those in *The Lord of the Rings*, both worlds consists of typography and the journey the characters make through it.

To get a visual of what I'm referring to, take a moment and examine the maps as they appear in each work:

Source: http://www.donsmaps.com/middleearthmap.html All credits to its creators.

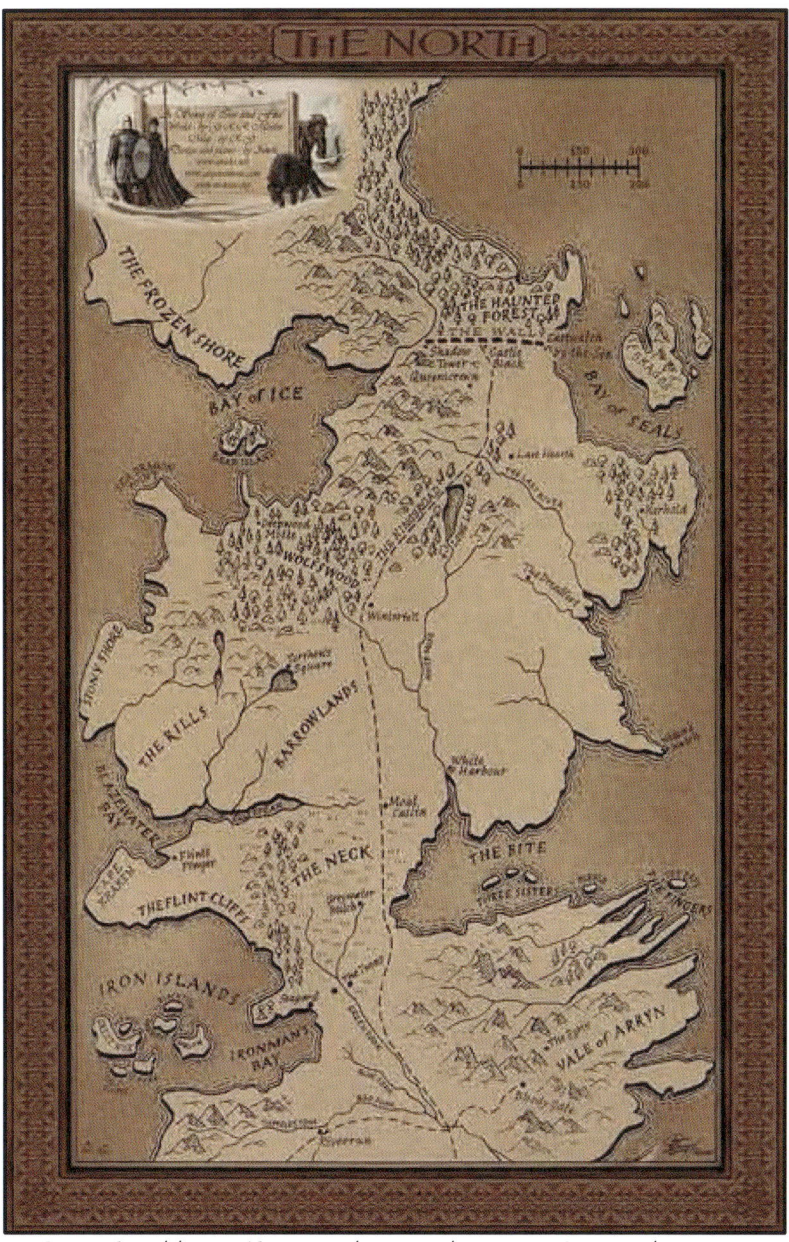

A STEP-BY-STEP GUIDE FOR WORLDBUILDERS

Source: http://gameofthrones.net/resources/50-maps-of-westeros/395-map-of-the-north.html All credits to its creators.

The first map above is from *The Fellowship of the Ring*, the first book in *The Lord of the Rings* series, and the second map is from *A Game of Thrones*, the first book in the *A Song of Ice and Fire* series.

In both creations you find the quintessential elements of fantasy maps present in the illustrations: angled mountains, rivers and coastlines, and both compass roses only indicate where north is. They also share a similar style with their pictorial design.

I purposely placed this example here to make you feel comfortable pulling out a small notebook, or a piece of paper, as you browse the Internet for fantasy maps. Every time you come across something you like, make a note of it without feeling guilt. Put it aside and repeat this exercise again the next day. Do this three times. I promise you, when you look over your scribbling on day three, ideas will begin to flow.

> Embrace it and know that you are on the right path.

SO DO YOU NEED A MAP?

I hope that what we have covered up until this point has both explained why maps are important, but also addressed some of the common excuses for not creating one. Above all, understand that a map tells a story on its own, and the very act of looking at one can fire up your audience's imagination.

There is merit in pursuing a level of *immersion* where the imaginary world feels as real as the one we are living in. For this reason, fantasy worlds and cartography have a very special relationship.

The first thing I look for when opening a fantasy novel is a map and if I don't find one… well, I'm already slightly discontented. The exact same thing could be said for opening a box with a new video game, or initiating a role-playing game. It all boils down to this question: Why deliberately force feelings of disappointment onto our audience when they are so easily avoided?

Fantasy stories and worlds are for exploration and all explorers need a map. That goes in real life as well as in fiction. Just imagine how you would feel if I parachuted you out over Greenland without any device to help guide you. Lost and confused, I would assume.

Understand how your audience might feel when you throw them into an imaginary world with no map to guide them. We cannot automatically expect them to follow along with all the strangely named places and still keep up with the story. The aid of a map makes a world of difference. It makes them believe that just over the horizon there is a functioning world. This is the illusion that maps help to create.

Maps provide an easy visual way to convey information to the audience which would otherwise have taken long and winding explanations. The magic needs to happen in the story as it unfolds, not as a backstory about why the mountain is called "Cold Peaks".

That would not be an exhilarating tale, but placing "Cold Peaks" on the map… now, we have something interesting. With just a glance, your audience will take in more of your world than you could ever explain to them while expecting them to stay awake.

I hope these introductory chapters have made you see just how important the addition of a map is to your fantasy world. Creating one is not only doable. With this step-by-step guide in hand, it also becomes a much less daunting task.

Don't let any excuses weigh you down.

Instead, know that your map might not be perfect, and it does take some practice, but your audience will still love you for it.

Are ready to let the *immersion* begin? Then let's dive in…

STEP ONE

※

SOMETHING TO CONSIDER

THINK, THEN ACT

If you have pen and paper at the ready, that's good – it will come in handy because you need to take some notes throughout this *Step One* of the map making process.

We are not quite ready to start drawing and have some ground to cover before committing lines to paper.

I find this a good time to make a point about worldbuilding.

At this stage, some of you will have completed parts of your worldbuilding, others will have almost everything done and organized in your filing system of choice, whereas the rest prefer to begin the entire worldbuilding process with the map itself. Now… it doesn't matter which category you belong to, and remember, we are all different: there isn't one right or wrong approach, yet we all face one fundamental truth.

Maps inspire story!

So this is where you should start you map creation process: with the understanding that the very first step is to think about the story you want to tell – whether a novel, a video game or a role-playing game.

If you were to jump straight ahead to the later stages of this book, you run the risk of spending time and energy on a map only to realize that you didn't think your creation through. At that point, all you can do is start all over. I would hate for that to happen.

Since this is a book on map making, and not plot or story creation, I will leave it to you to plan out your story, but at the same time, I don't want to leave you empty-handed. I have thus created a free worksheet that goes along with this book.

Download it from here:
https://www.jesperschmidt.com/fantasy-map-making-download/.

Note: If you are reading this book in paperback, then simply type the above URL into the browser on your computer and it will connect you to the download page.

The worksheet will not only serve as a checklist for the steps to come, but also provide you with inspirational questions when it comes to understanding which story elements are important to know.

A point to clarify before going further: I'm not implying that you need to plot everything out in minute detail. You just need to know a minimum: the basic concepts and essence of the wonderful tale you are about to let your audience experience. With the frame of your story clearly in mind, it's time to put that notepad to use.

In five short bullets, describe what elements are mandatory to have on your map in order to support your story. Try to distill the crux of *where* the events are to take place. For some, this will come easily, and others will have to spend some time mulling it over.

I might not have done as good a job as I could in explaining what I'm referring to by saying, "basic concepts and essence of the wonderful tale", so allow me to illustrate with an example.

These are the items I came up with when creating my map of Erisdün:

- I need an island continent to serve as the home for the "bad guys".
- I need a forest-covered area of the world, and it will be the only part of the world that has forest. No trees anywhere else in Erisdün.
- I need a Bronze Tower.
- I need an area that is completely frozen. A land of winter. (This became "The Northern Lands".)
- I need two large nations. They have to be neighbors and in direct opposition to each other.

Keep at it until you have nailed it.

You now have a very handy checklist of key elements that you will have to add to your map.

In order to arrive at this result, you *do* need to have a certain understanding of your story's elements. Without it, you can easily find yourself going down a rabbit hole.

The creation of a map can take many hours – of course depending on what you need it for and how professional you want it to look – and it would be a shame for all that work to go to waste. Worse yet, what if you have paid a designer or cartographer to make it for you?

Another, and much more famous, example of what I'm advocating in showcasing story aspects on the map can be found in J.R.R. Tolkien's *Middle-Earth*.

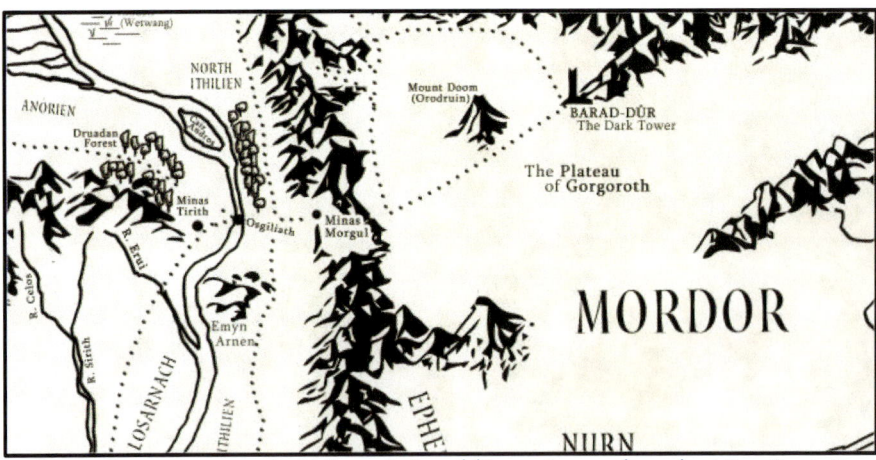

Source: Interactive map of middle earth, http://lotrproject.com/map/, All credits to its creators.

Take a second and study the location of Minas Tirith… Is it a coincidence that it's placed exactly where it is on the map?

No, far from it.

The name itself means "The Tower of Watch", and it is a fortress consisting of seven levels, each one rising one hundred feet above the one that comes before it. The lowest of the walls is the only one not white. It's instead made of black stone called Orthanc, and nothing but earthquakes can damage it.

Minas Tirith stands as a guardian against Mordor in the east, and protects Gondor and Rohan to the west.

This map design truly supports the story. It enhances it and creates the type of *immersion* we are looking to create.

I hope that you see how a great map will complement your story and how it plays a key role in fantasy. That said, I firmly believe that the story should always take priority. By that I mean never force your fable to take place at certain locations just because they accidentally made their way onto the map. If it's necessary to start over with a fresh map, then do so. It doesn't matter how painful a choice that may be. I have been there, so I know what I'm talking about.

Creating the setting itself belongs in a book on worldbuilding, but I mention it here because the better you understand your setting, the more you can improve your *understanding* of the world. As a result you can bring it to life on the map.

When done well, the landscape can itself take on the function of a character. When that happens it will give your audience a wonderful experience.

I wish I had thought of this very simple *Step One* for **Fantasy Map Making** much sooner.

It would have saved me much headache.

THE WISH LIST

Flip onto the next page of your notepad and we will continue with another short exercise. This one I call *The Wish List*.

It's to all intents and purposes an extension of the five bullet points of mandatory elements you just created.

For now think of *The Wish List* as an exercise in transforming your setting into places on the map. Consider where your characters could go. Where is it logical they would end up?

In doing so, keep in mind that you already know what your story is about at this stage. Your brain will automatically begin to form ideas, so allow your mind to wander and see what you can come up with. Your aim is to populate *The Wish List* with several unique places that will enhance your story and deepen the level of *immersion* for the audience even further.

Again, the story takes precedence. Don't force anything onto the map, or bend the tale you want to tell, just because your spur of creativity came up with a crazy idea.

I have here included my own *Wish List* from when I mapped my world of Erisdün. Sometimes examples speak louder than any explanation:

- I need a city that the "bad guys" can destroy. I added the city "Waters End".
- For contrast to the other nations, I need a society that lives underground. I added the Kingdom of Kraipia.

- I need a great, extravagant capital that shows how rich the expanding nation of the world is. I added the city "Naviot".
- The homestead of one of the main characters is called "Felistyr", but since it's a hidden forest city, I thought it made sense that these people would have a single city, visible to "outsiders", from where they could conduct trade. The city of "Eshe-Duin" was added to *The Wish List*.

All of the above points accommodated the story.

A good map will feature an interesting setting, and even if your map is nothing but a small town, you still need to challenge yourself to come up with something that is extraordinary about it.

If you are feeling stuck, then the inclusion of a terrain barrier – often in the form of a large inland lake – is always a go-to concept. Place it in the middle of the map and you have created a strategic barrier right at the center. Your boundary should be traversable, yet only through considerable effort. Hence, if you decide to use mountains instead of a lake, make sure that it includes dangerous passes. Other alternatives could be a vast desert only crossed by daring caravans, a glacier with deep pitfalls, or a swamp that turns into an impassable quicksand during parts of the year.

I should warn you that this is somewhat of a classic and could be considered a cliche solution. However, it still works when you add the major kingdoms around this shared point of reference. It gives the map a featured piece of terrain that draws all of your lands together into a thematic whole.

Whichever terrain barrier you decide on, if any, and no matter if it's seasonal or constant, do make sure that it's rippled with interesting details that beg for exploration.

Go ahead and complete your own *Wish List* and combine it with the five bullets from before.

Once you are ready, come back here, and we will move onto *Step Two* where we need to cover the topic of tools before getting any further…

A MENTAL NOTE

In closing *Step One* there is a final and important note to make.

Throughout the later stages of this book your map will begin to develop and, as it does, more and more details about your world will come into focus. It's very likely that the visual layout will add new ideas to your story. When that happens, challenge yourself to consider if these wondrous locations of isolated cities, underground caverns, hidden forests, volcanoes, pits, and lairs can somehow inspire plot twists.

What I said earlier still counts: story always trumps the map, not the other way around. However, why not make them work together and achieve the best of two worlds?

In relation to what I'm advocating here, I find this map from J.R.R. Tolkien quite interesting:

A STEP-BY-STEP GUIDE FOR WORLDBUILDERS

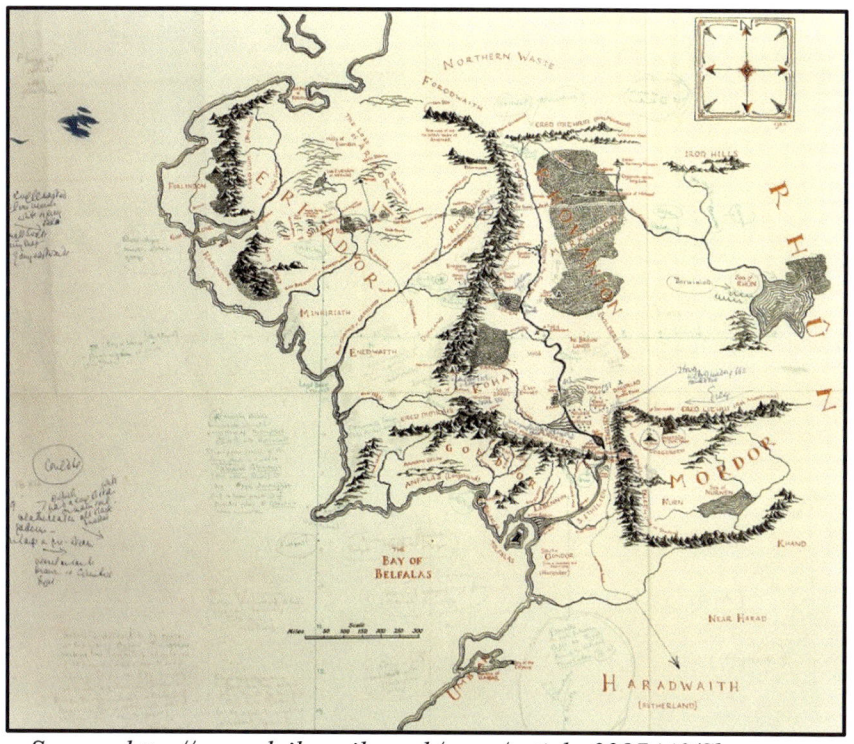

Source: http://www.dailymail.co.uk/news/article-3287440/Show-way-Mordor-Unique-hand-drawn-map-Middle-Earth-gives-rare-insight-Tolkien-s-mind.html All credits to its creators.

Although most of his hand-scribbled notes are adding additional details to each location, it shows the value of treating your map as a fluid entity. Keep considering it. Make adjustments whenever necessary. Promise yourself that until the map is ready for publication, or to be placed on the gaming table, you won't treat it as the final version. You should always be willing to move mountain ranges, rivers, cities or whatever it might be whenever your story demands it. Play with the ideas that arise and see where they take you.

Remember a couple of chapters back where I said, "When creating fantasy maps, I find it my job, as the creator, to maintain *immersion* by portraying the imaginary world in a way that, for the most part, is grounded in reality as we know it. To me a fantasy map is one that enhances the ability to captivate the audience's mind and let them accept the parts that are truly fantastic as nothing out of the ordinary."

Your audience will need to be able to interpret the information your final map conveys correctly. They have to understand it. One of the most effective ways to make your map visually appealing is to understand how geographical elements work in the real world. With this book to hand, you will be sure to go about creating your map with the necessary general understanding of geography.

Before we get that far, though, let's have a look at which tools we have at our disposal for map making.

Welcome to *Step Two*.

STEP TWO

TOOLS

YOUR TOOL OF CHOICE

There are different options when it comes to deciding which tools to use for your map making project.

Here in *Step Two*, I will cover the following:

1. Hand-drawing your map.
2. Using software to create your map.
3. Hiring a professional to do it for you.

One of these might already appeal to you and that is fine.

In the coming pages, I will give you some basic explanations of each one and allow you to decide your own preference. At the end of *Step Two*, I will give you my personal recommendation, but the best piece of advice to give is: *Go with your gut feeling*.

We all have different biases and no one tool is better than the others. They all come with pros and cons. The most important thing is that your choice makes the coming stages feel easy and enjoyable.

HAND DRAWN

My first map creations were on paper, made with pens and colored pencils, though I have to say that drawing is definitely not my strong suit. Furthermore, paper-based maps are harder to modify and to share with the world.

When you are starting out, you might find that hand-drawing is an essential first step before heading into software-illustrated maps. Know that in drawing a map, it's hard to make it look good unless you already have a certain skill level in that art.

If it's important to you that the final version of your map has a quality look to it, you might want to move on to the next section about software. If, on the other hand, you think that hand-drawing might be for you, here are some basics for you.

Note: If you are already an accomplished artist, you can safely skip ahead. You likely already know more than what I can tell you in this chapter.

When it comes to hand-drawing you need the following:

- Wooden pencil and/or mechanical pencil
- Ruler
- Eraser
- Paper

Pencils

Whether you work best with a wooden pencil or a mechanical one is a matter of personal choice, but when you use the mechanical version you won't need to sharpen it and the width of your lines will stay exactly the same.

Wood-cased pencils are, however, capable of much more expression and can be found in a greater variety of hardness. Since sketching and drawing are usually done with faster hand movements than technical drawing, it makes the balance of the pencil more important. The truth is that you may only discover whether a lighter or heavier pencil is right for you by experimenting. The same can be said for whether the weight of the pencil should lean towards the top or the center.

If you decide that the mechanical option is the one for you, I still recommend that you keep a wooden graphite pencil at hand for shading. The Faber-Castell 4B is a good option, as it is soft enough to give you a necessary variation between crispness and smudging. You could also opt for a carbon pencil, but it will give you more darkness and less shine than the graphite one.

Depending on the kind of map you choose to create, you may also wish to use colored pencils. As a beginner, there is no reason to start out with the big case of a hundred and fifty pencils, though. More is not merrier.

Research has actually proved that you become less satisfied with more choices. So, a good strategy is to go with a box of twenty-four or forty-eight pencils from a single brand. Select something available in open stock just to make it easier on yourself. Prismacolor Premier or Faber-Castell Polychromos are both good options.

At some stage you might begin to concern yourself with details like lead hardness. By then, you have surpassed the scope of chapter. For now, just try out a few pencils and find the one you prefer.

Ruler and Eraser

Regular gum erasers, like Staedtler, will work just fine. Their sharp corners can help define edges, and the rest of the body is easy to use and prevents messing up the drawing. You can also acquire mechanical erasers, but at a beginner's level I think that is an expensive route to take when you do not need to.

With rulers there are a few different options worth mentioning.

If how transparent rulers sometimes reflect the light bothers you, then a solid white ruler, which "blends in" with the white surface of the paper, might be a better option.

You can also take it up a nudge, by investing in a ruler that can be used to measure distances in either meters or miles. I admit that this is a bit advanced, and when you are just starting out it's not necessary. It's very neat how these rulers are designed for a specific scale of map.

You can find out more at: www.maptools.com/products/lat_lon_tools

On the front side, each one has minutes and seconds on one edge, and decimal minutes on the other. More importantly is the back side where it gives you distance and nautical miles.

These rulers are all printed on sturdy 20-millimeter plastic stock for durability and come in a variety of sizes to match the map you are creating.

Paper

I saved the topic of paper for last, because this is probably the most important one.

How do you decide what paper to get when you stand in front of aisles and aisles of different types at the store?

In essence, there are three things to consider:

1. What the paper is made of.
2. How much the paper weighs.
3. The surface quality of the paper.

Let's have a look at each one in detail:

1. What the paper is made of.

Because paper, for the most part, consists of cellulose – the base of all plant life – you can create paper from any kind of plant. This also means that each plant will generate a different kind of paper.

If you want to make sure that your drawing paper doesn't fade over time, you need to make sure that it doesn't contain any lignin (the organic polymer deposited in the cell walls of many plants, making them rigid and woody).

Most drawing paper is made of wood cellulose or cotton cellulose. When dealing with the wood version of the two, it originates from tree fibers, which contain lignin. The polymer is photoreactive, which means that it reacts to light. This is what causes the paper to become acidic and to discolor over time: think of newspapers that yellow fairly quickly.

However, when lignin is removed from the wood cellulose, you are left with a very durable paper.

So, how do you know how to avoid lignin?

Let's imagine that we are in the store, standing in front of all the different types of paper. What we are looking for are the ones labeled "acid-free" or "high alpha cellulose". The latter is code for *lignin-free*.

You might also see some papers classified as "pH neutral". Know that this does *not* mean that the paper is acid-free. It only points to the fact that it had a neutral pH value of 7 at the time of production. It can still become acidic over time.

I mentioned the cotton cellulose type of paper earlier. These are naturally lignin-free and are, at the same time, pH neutral. Because the paper is made from cotton fibers, it's also very strong. If you want to locate this type of paper, look for the label "100% cotton rag".

2. How much the paper weighs.

The weight of paper is determined at the pulping stage — it's rather complicated and there is no need to spell out the details here. All you really need to know is that you want paper that weighs around 200g/m2.

This gives you a strong, tough, and sturdy piece of paper.

3. The surface quality of the paper.

You will find that drawing surfaces can vary from ultra-smooth to very coarse. Which one is right for you really comes down to personal preference.

I can give you some indications as a starting point, though.

There are two main categories of surface quality: 1) hot-press paper; and 2) cold-press paper.

The first is smoother and has less texture because it has been pressed under heated, high-pressure cylinders, whereas the second is coarser and has more texture because no heat was used in its manufacture.

In essence, when you draw, the charcoal dust from your pen settles into the grooves created by the texture of the paper. Without the texture, the grooves would be too shallow and unable to hold the charcoal. This is where the personal preference comes in: do you like textured drawings better than smoother ones, or vice versa?

If you want some pointers on what type of paper to choose, here are a few: The "Strathmore 400" series is quite smooth and acid-free, or the "Stonehenge Drawing Paper", which is high-quality and made of cotton cellulose.

If hand-drawing maps is for you, then I recommend that you take the time needed to learn the techniques required. As with everything else you want to master in life, there are certain tips and tricks to follow if your map is to look real and of good quality.

You will find several good books on Amazon that will teach you what you need to know on how to draw maps. Another option is to search for *how to draw a map* on YouTube. It will produce a list of some excellent videos, made by craftsmen, which allow you to see the explanations put into action.

If hand-drawing is for you, you should feel excited about it by now. If not, or perhaps you are still undecided, then move on to the next section where I dive into the use of software.

SOFTWARE

There are lots of products on the market when it comes to software for map making and, for obvious reasons, I can't test them all. As you read through what is to come, know that the only program I have used myself, and still do, is Campaign Cartographer 3.

In building this list, I have focused on the most well-known programs, and recognize that, in the process, I have excluded a ton of options. So, this is not intended to be an exhaustive list, but an easy, digestible list to get you started.

In this chapter, we will look at the following software programs:

- Fractal Mapper
- Photoshop
- GIMP
- Adobe Illustrator
- Inkarnate
- Campaign Cartographer 3

NOTE: All mentioned prices are at the time of writing this book. Prices may change over time, so please visit the official website via the links provided below.

Fractal Mapper – http://www.nbos.com/products/fractal-mapper

This software allows you to create a wide variety of maps, ranging from small rooms to whole continents. It is fractal-based, as the name hints at, which makes for realistic coastlines, rivers and caverns.

You can create continent maps, city maps, dungeon maps, sci-fi deck plans on which you can place a hex grid, with or without numbering, if you prefer.

It also gives you a wide variety of print options, with the possibility to only print parts of your final map or even at a one-inch scale for gaming miniatures.

It is a high-powered mapping system with an easy to use interface. It also includes an add-on program called "Fractal World Explorer", which can be used for creating 3D-shaped relief maps and exporting them back into Fractal Mapper.

The software is priced at $34.95, and a trial version is offered.

Fractal Mapper runs on most modern Windows-based computers.

Photoshop – http://www.photoshop.com/products

This Adobe-produced software is incredibly powerful and can be used for so much more than just crafting maps.

It has the wonderful feature of layers, which are shared by the most powerful pieces of software. Campaign Cartographer 3 operates like this, too.

Layers allows you to create a stack of transparent sheets which you can draw on. They won't conflict with each other and you can move text around without messing up the image below. Or shift the position of a piece of terrain without affecting rivers and coastlines.

Once you are done, all layers can be merged into one whole map.

Photoshop is the premium solution, but it can also produce some incredibly beautiful maps once you get the hang of it. If you are interested, search the Internet for "Photoshop fantasy map". You will be amazed what this software can do for you.

It is priced as a monthly subscription plan at $19.99, and a trial version is offered.

The software runs on both Mac and Windows computers.

GIMP – http://www.gimp.org/

GIMP is a cross-platform image editor which can be used for multiple purposes, including map making.
Once again, this software operates using layers and is a strong alternative to Photoshop. It comes with a large array of quality functionality to create your own artwork, such as customizable brushes, filters and automatic image-enhancement tools. You can retouch images, crop, adjust color, and much more.
Whether you are a graphic designer or hobby illustrator, GIMP provides you with sophisticated tools.
It requires a certain level of effort to learn how to operate the software; however, the official website does provide some tutorials and the rest can be found on YouTube.
The best part is that it's open-source and complete free to use.
The software runs on both Mac and Windows computers.

Adobe Illustrator – http://www.adobe.com/products/illustrator.html

Adobe Illustrator has long been the standard when it comes to vector illustrations and designs.

Since a map largely consists of sharp lines and text, this is a very useful tool. Because it's vector-based, it supports scaling much better than Photoshop, and allows you to edit your lines point-to-point, which is extremely helpful when it comes to manipulating smooth curves.

The program allows you to create both free-hand drawings and import other graphics. Since Illustrator is an Adobe product it works seamlessly with the other Adobe programs in the Creative Suite, so you can even drag your creation into Photoshop for further editing.

The software is difficult to understand at first, but it should be well worth the learning curve.

It is priced as a monthly subscription plan at $19.99, and a trial version is offered.

The software runs on both Mac and Windows computers.

Inkarnate – http://www.inkarnate.com

This one is for all you RPG game masters out there.
Inkarnate is an RPG tool kit that allows you to create professional-looking fantasy maps.
It's in open beta testing, so all you need to do is sign up and play around with it. Know that functionality might be somewhat limited until the final product is ready.
If you intend to create commercial products, like a map for a book, you need a license which comes at a yearly price of $25.
Since the software is web-based, it does away with any system requirements.

Campaign Cartographer 3 – http://www.profantasy.com

As mentioned, this is the software I use. It is a truly powerful gem, but firstly I want to point out that it takes practice to master. Once you get the hang of it, though, it becomes quite easy and offers a ton of options with symbols, rivers, roads, text – you name it.

In terms of flexibility it is marvelous, and with this software you can create maps of anything from a cosmos, to worlds and individual rooms. It's in fact built with fantasy role-playing in mind, so it might be just what you are looking for.

Campaign Cartographer 3 is a solid choice and a point of reference for the whole map making market.

It is priced at $29.95, and a trial version is offered.

The software runs on most modern Windows-based computers.

⁂

Based on the short summaries above, I suggest that you pick the one that you find most interesting – or all, if you are up for it – and search for it on YouTube to see it in action. One thing is the quality of map that the software can produce, but having a user interface that appeals to you is not to be underestimated either. When you have made up your mind as to which you prefer, sign up for the trial version and take it for a test run before you complete the purchase.

Now, before I share my preferred approach to tools, let's look into one more option. This is where you do almost nothing and instead hire a professional cartographer.

HIRE A PROFESSIONAL

Whether or not you will want to hire a professional cartographer is largely dependent on the purpose of your map. If it's only intended for personal use, to keep track of places and their relative position to one another, then you might be better off just printing a copy or staying with your drawn version.

In case it serves as a companion to any published work, then I find it important to include a version that looks as good as you can possibly make it. Here the professional route might just be what you are looking for.

There are many great websites that will put you in direct touch with a professional cartographer. I have tried Guru (http://www.guru.com/) and Fiverr (http://www.fiverr.com) and can vouch for their credibility. It's definitely possible to find someone to make you a wonderful map and still stay within a reasonable price range. As an alternative, you can also advertise your needs on social media.

My intention is not to proclaim one website better than another. Besides, over time new ones will emerge and old ones disappear, but instead I want to share some general observations and considerations that you should keep in mind when making use of professional services.

If you downloaded the earlier mentioned free worksheet from here: https://www.jesperschmidt.com/fantasy-map-making-download/, you will now find the small surprise section I included helpful.

Once you have identified a designer whom you might want to work with, there are three things I recommend you to do before reaching out to the individual:

1. Read through the reviews submitted by other customers. It will give you a pretty good idea of both the person's design skills, and, equally importantly, how the person interacts with and treats his or her customers.

2. Search on the Internet for maps that you like. Save images or links. This way you can share them with the designer as a reference. Do not worry about copyright as this is only intended to put the designer on the right "style track" from the get-go. These images are not going to be used anywhere. Just like with maps, a picture paints a thousand words, so make it easy for both of you.

3. Use what you created during *Step One* and in a brief, concise manner explain to the designer what needs to be included on the map as a minimum.

With all those pieces ready, it's time to contact the designer and make necessary arrangements. For the most part, this is about agreeing on the price, but there are a few things worth mentioning:

1. Ask the designer how many rounds of editing/corrections are allowed within the agreed price. Later disagreements of this nature are not pleasant for either party. Better get it cleared right away and save you both a lot of headaches.

2. Agree what format and map sizes you will receive in the end. If you need it for a book, or similar, a smaller-scale version might be needed.

3. If you need the map for commercial purposes, e.g. you intend to sell the map as part of a published work or on its own, then make sure that the designer licenses all rights and ownership to you. Such a license should grant you all the copyrights and allow unlimited use in any context you see fit. In practical terms, this is just a one-page PDF document. Your designer should already know how to create one. If not, just search on Google for "License Agreement for artwork" and you will find templates. If

he or she declines to do this, then stay clear and find someone else. Simple as that.

Working with a professional cartographer can cost you anywhere from $5 to $500 – or even beyond.

As with everything else, you often get what you pay for, although in this next section I share what I have paid for different maps and will show you what the results looked like. Hopefully this gives you an impression of what to expect and also confirms that, even if you are on a budget, it's still possible to work with a professional and have a great-looking map created.

MY RECOMMENDATION

I hope the different options shared throughout *Step Two* have given you a better idea of whether hand-drawn maps, software or working with a professional is the better option for you. Which approach to take is a highly individual decision, and you should go with what suits your needs the most.

Next, I want to give my own preference because it gives me the opportunity to share specifics. I believe that showing you some different versions of the same map – my world of Erisdün – and how much each one cost me will in some way inspire or help you. These insights are best shared with pictures and practical examples anyway.

My personal approach is, in fact, a merger between the use of software and the use of a professional designer. Obviously, since I use my maps for fantasy books, working with a professional ensures that the final map is something I can proudly add within the first few pages of both eBooks and paperbacks.

As earlier mentioned, I use Campaign Cartographer 3 to produce my maps. The first version is just to show the cartographer what I want him or her to create. This is accompanied by some pictures of maps that I find on the Internet and like purely from a style perspective.

By creating a draft map first, I ensure that the map I'm commissioning is fully aligned with my vision for the story.

Here is what Erisdün looked like after the first pass:

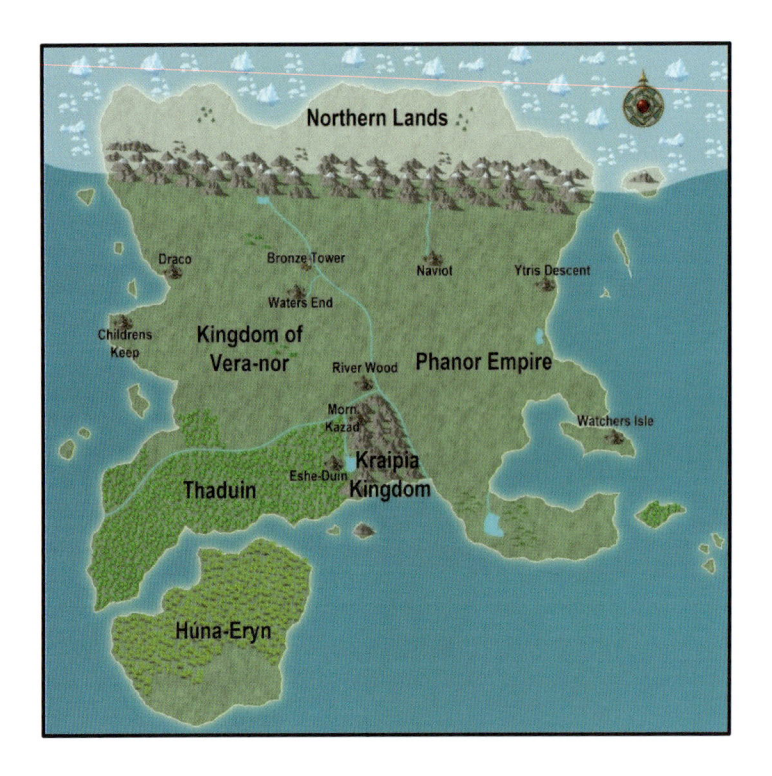

Author's note: As mentioned Campaign Cartographer 3 is not an easy piece of software to operate, so to give you all the tools and insight you need, I created a video series on my YouTube channel which shows you exactly how to go about using Campaign Cartographer 3. The videos are easy, understandable, step-by-step teaching. Here is the link, http://www.youtube.com/playlist?list=PL7pVHfk0zVX7656pEh86onQK5TqlV7jZW

I know that the above is far from a professional-looking map – yet.

What it does give me, and more importantly the designer, is a very clear understanding of the world. It's a sketch, and alongside it I hand over a one-page PDF which describes everything the cartographer needs to know about the world.

This was the content for Erisdün:

- The Northern Lands are a cold, icy and snowy. No one lives here. It's a harsh climate.
- The Kingdom of Vera-nor is the western nation. It has four major cities; Draco, Children's Keep, River Wood and Waters End. The lands consist mostly of open plains with hills here and there. It is important to note that there are no forests on these lands.
- The Phanor Empire is the eastern nation. It has three major cities; Naviot, Ytris Descent, and Watchers' Isle. The lands consist of open plains and hills in the northern part, whereas the southern part is swamplands and uninhabited. Important to note that there are no forests on these lands.
- The Bronze Tower is a huge bronze tower with a community of a few thousand inhabitants living around it. It's an independent piece of land that doesn't belong to either the Kingdom of Vera-nor or the Phanor Empire. Important to note that there are no forests on these lands.
- Thaduin is the southern nation. The lands are completely covered in massive and beautiful forests – beautiful beyond belief. It has only one city, which is Eshe-Duin.
- Kraipia Kingdom is the realm of the mountain people. The kingdom is wedged in between the other kingdoms and their domain covers only these southern mountains. One city is visible at the surface, and it's called Morn Kazad.
- To the south lies a jungle-covered island/continent called Hüna-Eryn. Evil dwells here in isolation from the rest of the world.
- I'm more than happy for you to put your own touches and ideas onto the map in order to improve its quality. Just be mindful to stick to the descriptions that I have listed here, as they link to the actual novel. Obviously, don't change the position of nations or cities.
- I have added two jpeg files of random maps I found on the Internet to give you an idea of what style of map I like.

This gives the designer a pretty strong understanding of what I want developed, and should do away with any misunderstandings. None of this is rocket science and it's merely applying a systematic approach.

I should mention that it's quite common to build a working relationship with a specific designer and you might find yourself coming back every time you need a new map. All things considered, this is actually my recommendation for a long-term goal. Before settling on one cartographer, though, try a few different ones. It gives you a point of reference as to the services you are paying for.

I hope you found this helpful and feel free to steal as much of this approach as you want.

In closing, I have below added the end results of what I got developed. In all cases, my initial crude map was transformed into something much better than what I could ever have dreamed of producing myself.

This first one was produced via Fiverr and cost me a total of $47.25:

A STEP-BY-STEP GUIDE FOR WORLDBUILDERS

This second variation was produced via Guru and cost me a total of $153.75:

This third and final version was drawn by hand and digitalized by http://www.sellswordmaps.com. It cost me a total of $400:

STEP THREE

※

THE

OVERVIEW

DESIGNING YOUR MAP

The remaining chapters are dedicated to the map making itself. Here is what we will cover:

- Step Four: Make a Sketch
- Step Five: Let There Be Land
- Step Six: Terraforming
- Step Seven: Islands and Lakes
- Step Eight: Rivers
- Step Nine: Forest
- Step Ten: Countries
- Step Eleven: Roads
- Step Twelve: Fantasy
- Step Thirteen: Final Touches
- Step Fourteen: Map Master

This is the order in which I approach all my map creations, and it's intended to make the process easy and logical.

So, without further delay, let's move on to the really exciting parts. As you work your way through each of the coming steps, keep this mantra in mind: spend as much time as you need on creating the map. If you rush it, the result will suffer. Relax. Have fun. And most importantly – tell your inner critic to keep quiet.

A map doesn't have to be perfect to have validity!

STEP FOUR

MAKE A

SKETCH

THE SIZE OF YOUR WORLD

Here in *Step Four*, I want you begin by determining the scope of your map.

By scope, I'm referring to deciding how large a map you are going to create. Do you plan to show an entire planet? If so, is it stretched out? Is it a hemisphere? Or do you need a single continent, a country, or just a city? Since you have already been through *Step One*, this should be fairly obvious and easy for you to determine.

In doing so, also consider what ratio between land and water suits your world the best. In most cases you will need to include both elements, but as a rule of thumb: for large-scale maps, show ocean(s), rivers, and lakes. For small-scale maps, display only a portion of same.

A common and easy path to take is to focus on one or two continents and then fill the rest with water. You can of course also head along the completely opposite route and create a map that mostly consists of water, with a few islands.

In a moment you are going to sketch a light framework to build upon in the later stages, and it will be important to strike a solid balance between land and water. If you have too much water, the map might end up looking uninteresting, whereas too much land could look strange and unrealistic. For the time being, just keep this in mind and I will come back to it shortly.

Evidently a map can never be as detailed as real-world maps, and when it's drawn on a piece of paper, it can suddenly seem so very small. This is the biggest question, and obstacle, here in *Step Four*. How do you get the size of your world just right?

You could be imagining a vast ocean with undiscovered land masses on the other side, or go as crazy as Terry Pratchett, when he made his world a flat disc which balances on the back of four elephants standing on a giant space turtle.

Source: http://legionofleia.files.wordpress.com/2015/03/discworld.jpg
All credits to its creators.

The point is this: To start a good map you need to decide upon scale.

There are no hard and fast rules on how big or small your world should be: this is fantasy, after all. You will want to keep your *Wish List* from *Step One* in mind, though, and then consider… traveling speeds.

This is a useful and very neat trick that goes a long way in tackling this part of the process.

In a fantasy setting you do not have cars or planes to take the characters around, so make sure that you don't create such an enormous world, rich in landmarks or cities, that your characters will never be able to travel the distances. As an example, know that even for *Middle-Earth*, which most people consider a large world, *The Lord of the Rings* trilogy takes place in a relatively small area. In most books, the distance from Bag End to Mount

Doom measures only a thousand miles. In contrast, there are 2445 miles between New York and Los Angeles.

So, how do you know what your map size should be? Well, let me give you some traveling distance tools.

WALKING

In the Middle Ages, the average healthy person could walk roughly fifteen miles a day.

They would have to stop for lunch and shortly before dark to find shelter and mount defenses against bandits. If nutritious food and smooth terrain were available, a man could push himself to cover thirty miles in a day. Yet such a pace would only be possible for a few days. When terrain turned rough, it would seriously reduce progress, as would any time spent on hunting and gathering food.

Peasants who commuted to and from the fields every day would normally be limited to a trip of two or three miles. This is why many villages in the Middle Ages would only be a few miles apart.

On paved roads, a trained, running messenger could cover thirty miles in about nine hours. This is not for your average Joe, though. In comparison, Roman soldiers on the march averaged about twenty miles per day, and only when they benefited from a long hours of daylight.

As a rule of thumb, you should calculate "a good day's walk" as ten miles.

ON HORSEBACK

With a horse, it becomes an entirely different matter and range increases dramatically, especially in rugged terrain.

As on foot, endurance and health do have a role to play, but in general you are looking at thirty miles a day when riding. That really makes the running messenger that more impressive, doesn't it?

You could push and reach sixty miles in a day, but a horse could only keep up that kind of pace for a short duration. Maybe for a couple of days at the most.

Horse stations would not be uncommon, and because they provided the option of changing steeds, the traveling distance could be increased to almost a hundred miles a day. They were often used by royal messengers.

ON WHEELS

The use of carts was usually an instrument of transportation. Moving things like coal, armor, or hay was an uncomfortable and slow mode of transport. For this reason even coaches often only carried the driver, controlling the six to eight horses pulling the weight.

This way of traveling would only get you twelve miles a day and that was when it didn't break down. Which it did, often.

It was slower than walking, but what you lost on speed you gained in range, since you could bring your own supplies and circumvent the need for foraging. Trade caravans are a great example, but even those would be greatly affected by both terrain and weather conditions.

BY BOAT

This was likely the fastest method to get around during the Middle Ages.

You would obviously be dependent on things like the current, tides, wind speeds – not to mention the type of sails used.

However, to keep things simple, I advise to use one hundred miles a day as your calculating average.

AND THERE WAS MAGIC

And since this is fantasy, we should not forget how magic can greatly speed things up, too.

If you have read Robert Jordan's *Wheel of Time*, you will know about Waygates.

These constructs are perfect examples of what I'm thinking of here. These things allowed the characters to cover massive distances in a single day – if they survived the trip, that was. Portals, like the Waygates, are ways in which you don't need to feel the limiting constraints of distance.

FINISHING THE SKETCH

I'm confident that this gives you a good sense of what would be a realistic span for your map.

You now know what size of map you need. You understand which key elements are needed, as dictated by your *Wish List*, and you can now make the necessary decision on what ratio of water and land is needed to support this vision of the world.

There is no need for details at this stage. You only need to create a crude sketch – and I mean really crude. Use pen and paper and just let your imagination flow; in fact, the more tiny curves and inlets you create, the better off you will likely be.

Also, it doesn't matter what it looks like, and you might throw several versions into the bin and start over. The purpose of this sketch is to help you to orientate before you spend time on specifics only to discover that you have ended up contradicting what you laid out in *Step One*.

Draw out a few quick sketches and see what suits you the most. I usually focus on outlining the land masses and getting the size of the world fairly accurate. This also tells me where I need water, and if a terrain barrier was added in the form of a water passage, as covered in *Step One*, it will also allow for fast transport from one end of the map to the other, increasing the characters' reach in the realm.

Remember: this is a rough sketch, so there is no need to labor it. Just do enough to give yourself an idea of scale, land and water. When you know what you want to do with your map, life will become much easier in the steps to come.

With that all sorted, another useful thing to consider is the style of map you are going for, since it might change the way you outline or draw it. A geographical map, a political division of the land, or a simple road map will all look different and include different elements. Just make it clear in your own mind what you will be going for as the final result, and, in doing so, know that what you leave out is every bit as important as what you put in. You could, for instance, choose not to include a southern coastline and simply let it fade off the paper.

What I am getting at here is that it's worth considering only to map out the parts relevant to the story you want to tell. So, when you are sketching a country, or a continent, stop once in a while and ask yourself, "Am I drawing this shape because I need it?"

That is the power of sketching.

Let your hand run wild and then edit yourself until you are happy with the results.

When you are ready, move on to Step Five…

STEP FIVE

LET THERE BE

LAND

TECTONIC PLATES

With your sketch all done, you have a solid aim for what you are going for. It's now time to produce the map itself.

A good working unit to start with is the continent. More often than not, fantasy stories are set on a single continent, but if your world needs several, just apply this step to each one.

For a start we need to understand tectonic plates.

WHAT ARE TECTONIC PLATES?

When talking about tectonic plates we are referring to the Earth's lithosphere, but luckily we only need to understand the very basics in order to produce a fantasy map.

To put it into context, though, the uppermost part of the lithosphere is called the crust. It reacts chemically to the atmosphere, hydrosphere, and biosphere and thus creates soil. Underneath is the mantle, which is weaker, hotter and deeper.

A graphical representation might work the best:

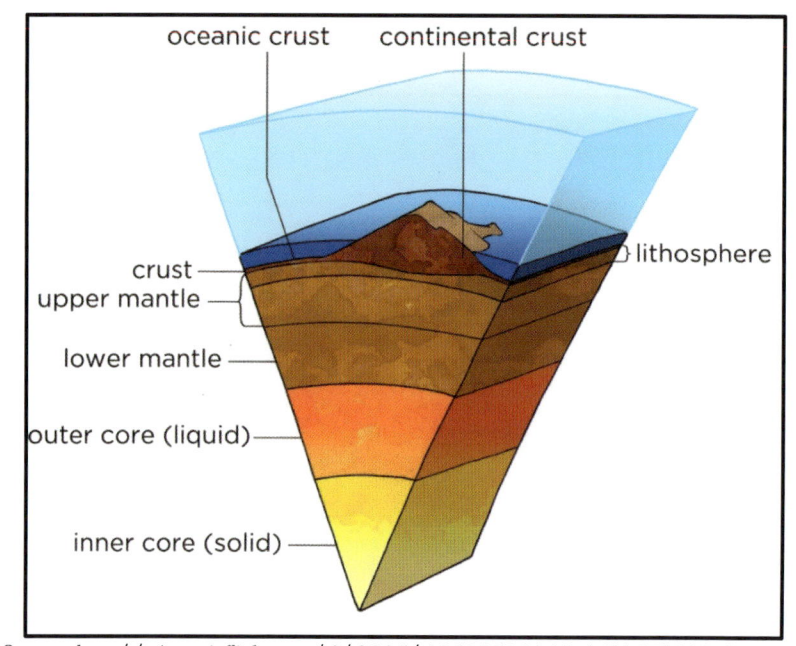

Source: http://c1.staticflickr.com/3/2825/13598528144_b6bb57b333_b.jpg All credits to its creators.

The outer shell of the Earth is broken up into tectonic plates which sit on top of the crust and separate the livable land from the molten lava underneath. On Earth we have seven major plates: Africa, Antarctic, Eurasian, Indo-Australian, North America, Pacific, and South America. There are also a number of smaller plates, but for the purpose of map making we will ignore these.

Your tectonic plates will in most cases consist of a mixture of oceanic and continental crust, but you can of course also create one similar to Earth's Pacific Plate where there is no continent present. We are most interested in plate movements, though.

It's the differences in temperature that cause lava to flow and move underneath the surface, which is the source for the tectonic plates shifting positions. It all happens very slowly, with these massive plates of rock moving up to 3.9 inches per year.

As they move, one of three things can happen:

1. They separate, which causes new crust to be created. This is what causes canyons and valleys to appear on the surface.

2. They collide. One tectonic plate will slide beneath another and push it upward. When there is a continent involved, it will form mountains, and in the ocean volcanoes can create chains of islands.

3. Or they simply slide past each other. Because of the massive forces at play, that causes what is known as a continental fault. The San Andreas Fault is a great example. It extends roughly 750 miles through California and forms the tectonic boundary between the Pacific Plate and the North American Plate.

Here is what the San Andreas Fault looks like:

Source: http://c1.staticflickr.com/1/9/15392616_db43e7487e_b.jpg. All credits to its creators.

Since we can only inspect one planet thoroughly, namely Earth, there is no way of judging how much variation there is in plate sizes and shapes. On our planet they tend to be roughly square in form, which is a good starting point when it comes to map making.

In *Step Four*, I had you create a rough sketch of your world and with this basic understanding of tectonic plates and how they move, we are in a position to simplify the process enough to make it easy on ourselves. If you wanted to, you could of course simulate the evolution of your planet and how various supercontinents, similar to Pangea from which the plates of Earth originate from some 250 million years ago, may have formed and broken up over time. Such events would have crafted older mountain ranges, like the Appalachian Mountains, which many scientists believe to be the oldest in the world. While this would certainly give you a very realistic map, I find it too excessive for the vast majority of us worldbuilders.

Instead, divide your rough sketch into a number of plates and decide which direction they are moving in. Use the three different options mentioned above and then make a note of the consequences: where will there be deep canyons, high mountain ranges, and faults? This will help you form a much more realistic map.

This is indeed simplifying matters, as the underlying mechanisms on Earth are much more complicated than that. Things like the size and composition of our planet, its magnetic fields, oceans, and the rather large moon might all be factors that caused plate movements here on Earth that we don't find happening in a similar fashion on Venus and Mars.

Let's get an example map going for the remaining steps of this book.

ADDING TECTONIC PLATES TO YOUR WORLD

S o, here we are:

A rough sketch on which I have marked my tectonic plates by the use of dotted lines.

As you can see, this is just a quick, hand-scribbled draft – as any sketch should be. I now decide that the two tectonic plates are pushing against each other. Hence, I will need to add mountains along the edges of my two plates.

It's now time to transform this rough sketch into a map. In my case, this means that I will transition into screenshots from the Campaign Cartographer 3 software. If you decide to hand-draw your map, or use a different piece of software, get that going now.

You should draw coastlines first. Work outward and around from that starting point. In order for the map to look realistic, remember that coastlines are very irregular and fractal. Also, add inlets and bays, as these will create a lot of variance to your coastline. The bays can be kept quite irregular, as they are part of the coastline, whereas the inlets are just smaller wedges or pockets of water that trail into your continent.

This electronic version is not a perfect replication of the sketch, but it will do for instructional purposes. You, on the other hand, should of course take the time needed to make it accurate. With your continent(s) drawn up, leave it at that. Keep the notes you just made on mountains, canyons and faults close by, but do not apply them to your map just yet.

STEP SIX

TERRAFORMING

WHAT ARE CLIMATE ZONES?

Terraforming your world, or creating the climate, can be a terribly complicated subject.

Just consider the Bodélé Depression for a moment: it's a valley on the southern outskirts of the Sahara which was once a lake bed. It has since dried out, but the dust is full of nutrition from the micro-organisms that used to live there. Every year, from October to March, the wind comes in from the east, and as the velocity picks up, it blows the dust across Africa, over the Atlantic, before it reaches the Amazon rainforest and fertilizes it with 40 million tons of dust. It's quite amazing.

This level of complexity is found everywhere on Earth, and that is also why it's so hard for even climate experts to predict how global warming will affect a particular place or a specific species. There are just too many variables.

For the purpose of fantasy map making we, however, do not want to spend days mulling over climate models. Instead, we are looking for a simplified approach to define the climate, and with your continents in place this is a good time to do just that.

While the goal isn't to emulate Earth, it's still a good starting point. Our planet is divided into three major climate zones: polar, temperate, and tropical.

Here is what it looks like on a heat map:

A STEP-BY-STEP GUIDE FOR WORLDBUILDERS

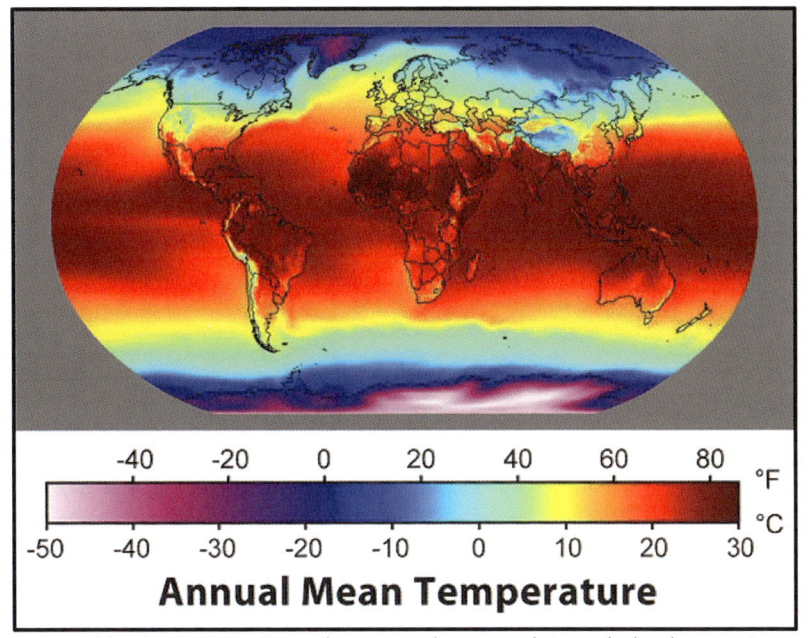

Source:http://upload.wikimedia.org/wikipedia/commons/thumb/a/aa/Annual_Average_Temperature_Map.jpg/622px-Annual_Average_Temperature_Map.jpg All credits to its creators.

The bluish areas represent the Poles, the lighter blue to turquoise are the temperate areas, whereas the red shows the tropical regions.

Go back to your rough sketch – the one I had you mark tectonic plates on during *Step Five* – and determine where the Equator is situated on your map. And remember: the Equator can also run outside of the map edges.

No matter where you place the Equator, its position not only determines where areas of green, your tropical band, are placed, but also gives you an idea of where the temperate and polar regions are located.

What kind of climate your map needs is of course dependent on the story you are going to share. If hot areas are a necessity, then keep the Equator fairly close; if not, place it far away and include a cold climate on your map.

In case you are creating a map of an entire world, I would strongly suggest that you include all three climate zones, because it offers the most varied array of locations, people, and possible monsters for your setting. Besides, it's what the audience will expect to find, so there is no reason to break *immersion* on this note.

With climate zones defined, there are a number of items which now lock themselves in place. So, let's investigate each one and let it feed into the map…

ADDING CLIMATE ZONES TO THE MAP

Since our planet is divided into three major climate zones, as shown on the heat map just before, the different regions of the map will also be affected in bands of latitude.

But how do we easily work out where to include rainforest, wide plains, ice Poles etc.?

Let's begin by viewing another picture. This will make the coming explanations so much easier:

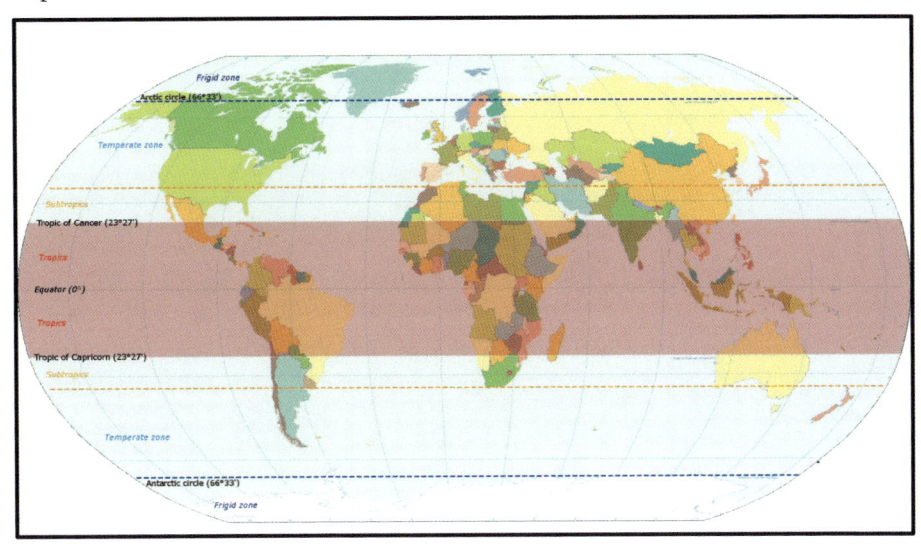

Source:http://upload.wikimedia.org/wikipedia/commons/b/b0/World_map_indicating_tropics_and_subtropics.png All credits to its creators.

Below we are going to work from the Equator and outward. In the process we will investigate each type of biome (very large ecological areas on Earth's surface) which you can expect to find at each band of latitude. For reference, the Equator sits at 0° latitude, and the North Pole at 90° North.

❧❦

Along the Equator and out to about 10° – here you will find areas with rainforest. It will have heavy rainfall throughout the year, and temperature variations are limited. The soil is poor with minimum underbrush.

There will be a high level of biodiversity with no one type of trees, plants or animals in domination.

You will also find monsoon areas, where short seasons of dryness will follow long wet ones. Here, the forest is not quite as dense, and there will be more ground cover. This is all caused by reversing wind patterns which I will explain shortly, but for now just make a note that, because of the monsoon, you have the possibility to change the scenery slightly if you prefer.

❧❦

At the 20° band – long dry seasons are followed by short wet seasons. For this reason the typical vegetation is scrub with isolated trees. It's here that you find the Savannah.

High temperatures are still the norm and the sun can beat down from directly overhead once or twice each year.

At the 30° band – this is where deserts are found. Rainfall will be minimal and plant life will, for the most part, be limited to cacti and shrubs. Temperatures are obviously still high, but it can grow quite cold at night.

There are some further details to consider when dealing with desert. I will soon come back to that and give you all you need to know.

❧❦

Between 30° and 45° – subtropical regions are found at these latitudes. Think of places like the Southern US and Southern China, where you are exposed to direct sunlight for a large part of the year. Summers are humid, around 70 and 80° Fahrenheit (20-30° Celsius), and winters are mild, around 45 and 50° Fahrenheit (7-10° Celsius).

Forests and grasslands are the most common type of vegetation.

On the eastern side of these continents, like Eastern Europe or most of California in the US, transitional zones might form into Mediterranean areas. As a consequence, the summer will turn dry and winters mild and rainy.

In terms of vegetation, you will now see evergreens and fruit trees such as olives and citrus. Shrubs and grass will also be widespread as they have adapted to survive the summer drought. This kind of climate is very important when it comes to agriculture, and if you have it on your map, this could very well be where you will add lots and lots of farmlands.

If we move the focus to the western side of these same continents, summers turn mild and rainy, while winters are relatively warm. Places like the Pacific Northwest and Northern Europe are examples. Unless it has been deforested by human activity, woodlands will be a common sight, too.

෴

Between 50° and the Arctic Circle – this is the largest land-based biome on Earth and it's called the taiga. It's mostly covered by coniferous forest (evergreen trees with needles).

The soil is very poor and has little undergrowth. Summers are muggy and brief, with temperatures averaging around the freezing point (32°Fahrenheit or 0° Celsius). Winters are extremely cold. Consider Siberia where the temperature drops to -49° Fahrenheit (-45° Celsius).

Moving further north, to the North Pole, we find the tundra. This is the coldest of all the biomes on Earth. The word 'tundra' actually comes from the Finnish word, *tunturia*, which means 'treeless plain'. And that is exactly what it is. The soil is permanently frozen and the landscape is uniform in appearance with the complete absence of trees, and has permanent ice coverage.

Up here the temperatures are extremely low and vegetation is limited to lichens and mosses.

❦

With the above descriptions of each biome, coupled with your previous decision on where the Equator is placed – on or outside your map – you now know what summers, winters, soils and vegetation will look like on your lands.

Each of these zones is enabled by the axial tilt of your planet, which in astronomy is expressed as the angle between the planet's rotational axis at its North Pole and a line perpendicular to the orbital place of the planet. Today, the Earth's axial tilt is 23.5°, but this tilt varies between 22.1° and 24.5° during a cycle that averages 40,000 years.

The axis is tilted in the same direction throughout the year, but as Earth orbits the sun, the hemisphere (half part of Earth), tilted away from the sun, will gradually come to be tilted towards the sun and vice versa. This is what causes our seasons: summer and winter.

So, unless you are going for an off-world setting, I would advise you to keep the tilt of your planet aligned with that of Earth. It not only makes things simpler, but the axial tilt of Earth is also close to the optimal value for the development of advanced life. You also need a moon to function as a stabilizer. This is what keeps your planet's tilt fairly constant.

On the other hand, if you are considering an alien setting, you can find inspiration in Mercury and Uranus. Here the tilt angle is zero for the former, and 90° for the latter.

Both of these extremes produce drastic temperature differences across the planet, and scientists believe that a planet without a tilt would be stratified into climate bands that would get progressively colder as you moved away from the Equator. The ability to survive the continuous winters at the higher latitudes would be impossible. Hence, if you are aiming for this type of planet, you should have the population congregate at the planet's tropical mid-section.

Let's return to the example map which we begun in *Step Five*. This is what it looks like when we apply all the different latitude bands:

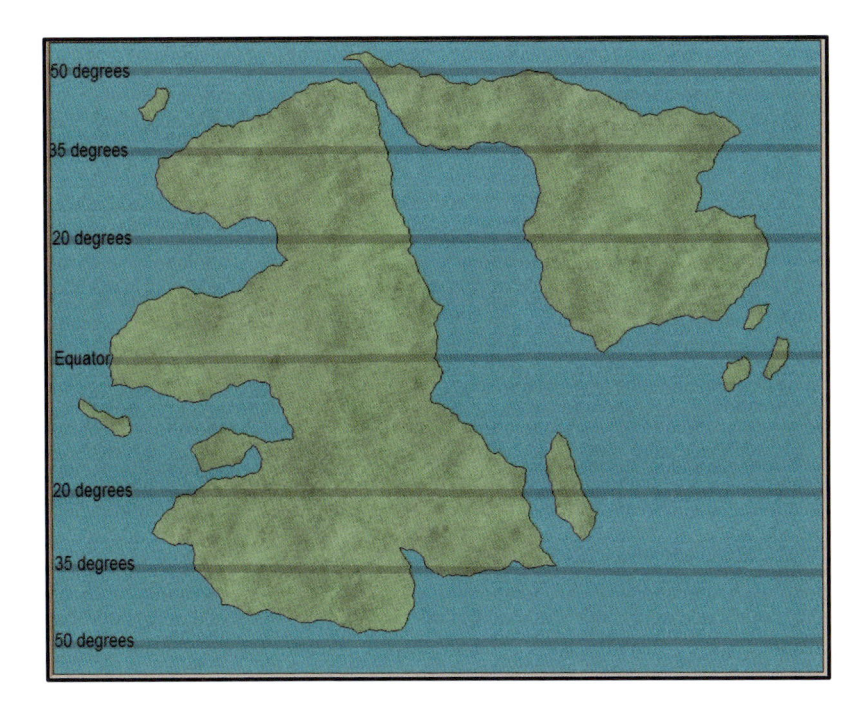

Above, I assumed that it was a map of a whole world and marked out the Equator at the center of it. This would automatically tell us the climate of each area across the map. It's of course possible to move the Equator up or down, or even off the map, and apply the effects accordingly.

As this example shows, you need a fairly big scale if you want to build a world map. Without it, the different zones of your planet get cramped together quite easily and, as mentioned earlier, for fantasy maps it's often best to work in a single or two continents.

When we next return to our example map, I will thus have stripped away the above latitude bands. Instead, I will assume that the Equator runs somewhere north, outside the border of the map, and the world portrayed in our example sits in the 30-45° climate band. The reason being that, in most cases, the scope of your map will fall inside one latitude band. As an additional positive, it also makes the coming examples less complicated as we move through the coming chapters.

Next, we are going to look at weather patterns, but before heading there, make sure you have decided upon the position of the Equator for your map and made notes of the high-level climate details mentioned above.

WEATHER PATTERNS

The whole atmospheric engine – the polar, temperate and tropical climate zones – only deals with heat, and we also need to consider rainfall. Weather patterns will designate certain physical aspects of your map and are thus very important to the process of map making.

The focus of this chapter is to understand how moist air is carried around your map, because this knowledge is needed when we next deal with a particularly important part: deserts. We will come back to that soon, but for now let's focus on the dampness of your world.

While rain *does* depend on heat levels, we are going to look at the lower atmosphere in three convection cells (self-contained areas where the upwards motion of warmth in the center is balanced by downward motion of cold at the periphery) which are found between the Equator and the Pole. They are called the Hadley cell, the Ferrel cell, and the Polar cell.

As always, a picture speaks a thousand words, and so here is what it looks like:

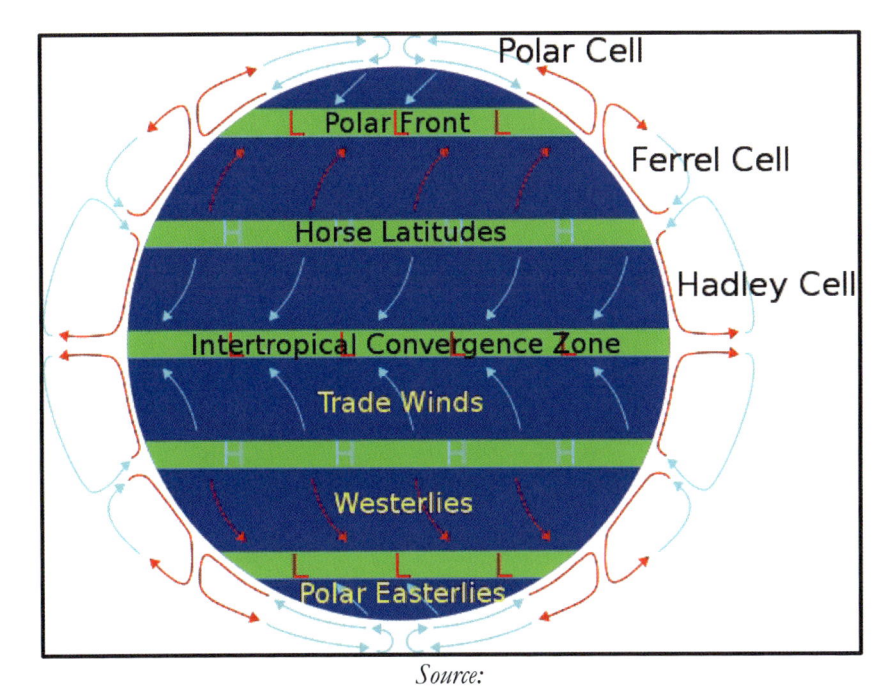

Source:
http://upload.wikimedia.org/wikipedia/commons/thumb/7/79/Atmospheric_circulation.svg/602px-Atmospheric_circulation.svg.png All credits to its creators.

The main driver of weather is the sun, and it warms the air at the Equator until it's heated enough to rise and move towards the Poles and eastward at a height of 7 to 9 miles (12 to 15 km). Here it becomes cooler and sinks at a latitude of about 30° until it returns along the surface toward the Equator and westward. This is the Hadley cell, and because the air is moist at the Equator this is also where we find rainforest.

In the Ferrel cell, the overall movement is the opposite of the Hadley cell, so here we are traveling poleward and eastward along the surface. This cell is weaker in its structure and the winds within are frequently interrupted, leading to the more fickle weather conditions of the temperate climate zone.

Lastly, the Polar cell. Relatively warm air rises at around 60° and moves poleward and eastward at a height of 5 miles (8 km). When it reaches the Pole it will cool off, drop in altitude, and move towards the Equator and westward along the surface. As a consequence, the air is dry, so this area will have very little rainfall.

If, for a brief moment, we return to the notion of building an off-world setting, then know that the above mentioned 30° and 60° latitude marks vary depending on either the rotation speed or the warmth of the planet. The faster it rotates, or the hotter it is, the larger the Hadley cell will become. On Venus, with a surface temperature of nearly 1200° Fahrenheit (467° Celsius) the Hadley cell will reach 60° latitude, causing a vast expansion of the "tropical climate zone".

In closing, consider your ratio between land and water that I mentioned back in *Step Four*. If you decide to have a world consisting mostly of water, you are unlikely to find very arid regions. On the other hand, in a setting which largely consists of land, there isn't going to be much rainfall.

The one exception is the monsoon, caused by reversing wind patterns. On Earth the best-known areas affected by the monsoon are India, Indonesia and Australia, where winds blow northeast in the summer, bringing rain. Monsoon areas depend on the differing heat capacity of oceans and continents, which means that they will appear where you have ocean at the Equator and a continent to the north or south around the 30° band.

While the above doesn't necessarily give you details to add onto your map, it does give you ideas which you can share when your audience experiences your setting. Role-players might face heavy rainfall during Monsoon, video gamers could potentially be subjected to fickle weather conditions in the Ferrel cell, and characters in a book are perhaps wishing for just a few raindrops as they move about the Hadley cell.

This is all helpful information that allows you to portray the climate in a realistic way, and, more importantly, it lays the groundwork for where we are heading next.

MOUNTAINS AND DESERTS

Back in *Step Five*, I had you make some notes on where mountains, canyons and faults would occur, and in my example sketch, I decided on two tectonic plates that push against each other.

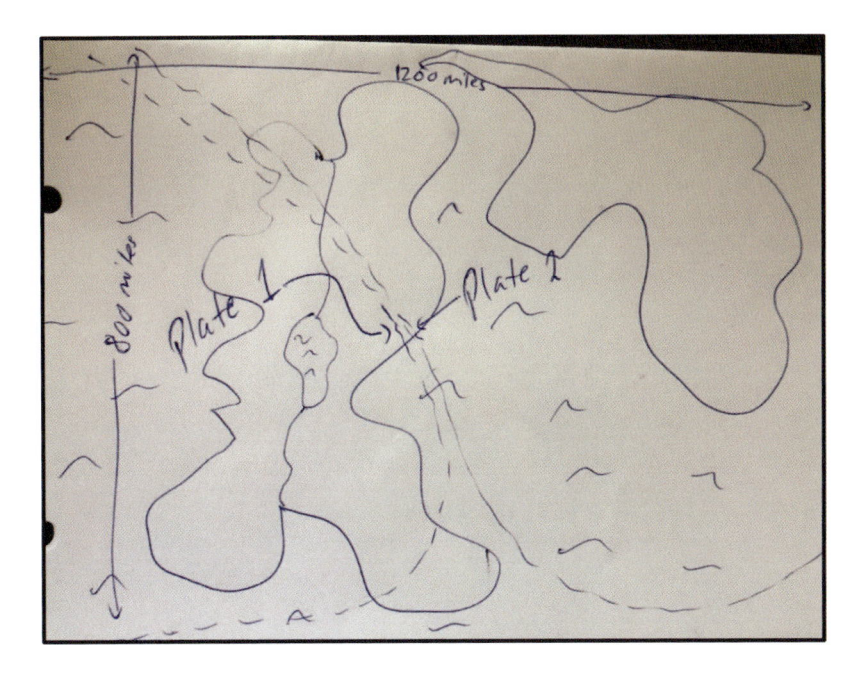

This also means that I will need to add mountains to the map where these plates meet – at the dotted line in the middle of the above drawing.

When it comes to mountains, they will always form in a long, strung-out, rough line. If, for some reason, you would like to add mountain ranges in 90-degree angles to one another, where one is north-south and the other east-west, then avoid putting them next to each other. As covered in *Step Five*, the tectonic plates would not produce mountains in such a formation. Neither would you see mountains form in a circle or something crazy like that.

In terms of width, mountain ranges can be very thick – as in 20 or 40 miles – but their smaller cousins, the hills, are just as important and will usually be located very near mountains. Newly formed ones have jagged tops because they form straight up from the tectonic plates underneath and push older mountains outward. So, in adding mountains to your map, make sure you place the jagged ones in the center of the mountain range with older ones at the edges. The latter will have rounded-down peaks.

Mountains serve perfectly as physical and political borders. You can develop a full continental divide that separates the continent with a line of mountains, either running north to south (splitting your continent into a left and a right half) or east to west (splitting your continent into a top and a bottom half). However, making the divide traverse the entire region is not always the best idea. It isolates areas of the map, making it difficult for the characters to reach those places. In the sketch above, I purposely made sure that the terrain barrier only carved out the north-eastern part of the continent, leaving the rest of the map open for easy exploration. Whichever approach you prefer, you should make the divide "sway" from side to side along the edges of the tectonic plates to increase realism.

In adding a continental divide, I also recommend that you let it run north to south, instead of east to west, due to climate zones. Moving north and south will expose the characters to different kinds of terrain and climates, whereas an isolating boundary from east to west will force your characters to stay in a very similar environment. It just makes your setting less interesting overall.

A few real-world examples of continental divides would be the Rocky Mountains of North America, dividing the continent into a western third and an eastern two-thirds. Similar to that are the Andes of South America, which also run north to south, whereas the Alps of Europe divide the continent diagonally.

You will find the same present in famous fantasy maps, like that of *Middle-Earth* or The North from *A Song of Ice and Fire*. Each one makes use of the continental divide, too. In these examples the divide acts as a barrier that holds evil forces at bay. In *Middle-Earth* the mountains of Ered Lithui and

A STEP-BY-STEP GUIDE FOR WORLDBUILDERS

Ephel Dúath offer protection against Mordor. In Westeros, The Wall equally separates the rest of the world from giants, Wildlings and White Walkers.

Mountain ranges such as these are a hugely important element to fantasy maps. Apart from all we have covered so far, they will also determine the direction of your world's rivers (we will come back to that in *Step Eight*) and they add a sense of vastness when volcanoes pop up here and there. Volcanoes can basically form anywhere on a tectonic plate from plumes of molten rock, so it's often a good idea to add one or two.

As you establish your natural barriers – be it a full continental divide or just separating out a corner of the map – ideas might begin to form as to what cultures and races exist on the other side of those mountains. Make a note as soon as such thoughts occur and add it to your worldbuilding notes.

With mountains, our example map now looks like this:

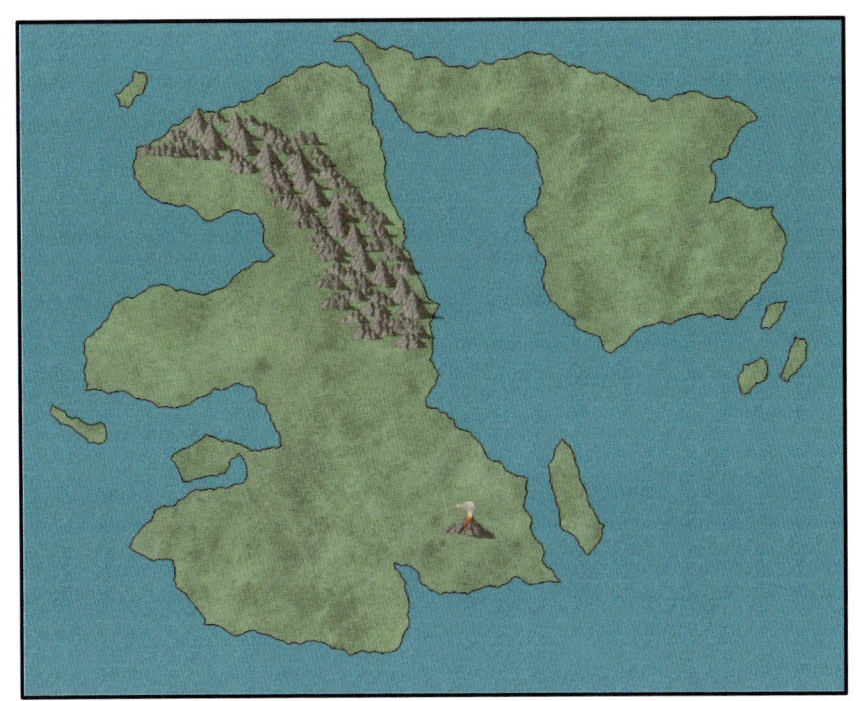

As you can see, I have made sure to place mountains with jagged tops at the center of the mountain range which runs along the line I decided represented where tectonic plates push against each other. Mountains with more rounded tops have been placed on both sides and, for flavor, I also incorporated a volcano in the southeastern corner of the map. From the previous chapters,

I also know that the climate across my map will be subtropical (remember how this example map sits in the 30-45° climate band), and since we just covered the topic of weather patterns, let's apply that knowledge now.

The point of the previous chapter was to learn how moist air was carried around the map and in following that logic here, it will tell you where not only deserts will be found, but also fertile grounds. As earlier mentioned, deserts form at the 30° band, but I needed to cover weather patterns before I could explain why.

Due to the world's airstreams, the outer edges of the Hadley cell will have air descending at a latitude of about 30°. Here the air will be much more stable and have fewer clouds. In other words, less rain is produced, and as a result you will find very dry climates: deserts.

As storms travel west inside the Hadley cell, and deposit water as they go from sea to land, the eastern coast of your continent won't have desert, and even if your land mass is thin, like the lower half of South America (around 30°), you will only find deserts on the western coast.

Another way to look at the same thing is to consider that the trade winds inside the Hadley cell blow towards the west and when they hit mountains, they will let rain fall. In doing so, they create a environment with fertile lands on the eastern side of the mountains, while the western area is left barren and desolate. This phenomenon is often referred to as a "rain shadow" and this is where deserts exist. Think of the arid west coasts of Mexico, Peru and Australia.

If your map sits inside the Ferrel cell, then winds go in the opposite direction, towards the east. This is what creates the natural cycle in the North Atlantic where you can travel west from Europe in the southern latitudes, and return home using a more northern route. Since winds vary more here, you can decide to have a rain shadow on the eastern coast if you prefer.

This logic might be slightly simplified, compared to the complex environment on Earth, but for fantasy map making it's more than enough to give your creation a very realistic feeling.

Again, returning to our example map, I decided to place us in the 30-45° climate band, so I will consider it within the Hadley cell. Had it been in the 45-60° climate band, I would have decided to operate by the standards of the

Ferrel cell instead. The Polar cell is obsolete when it comes to placing deserts – obviously.

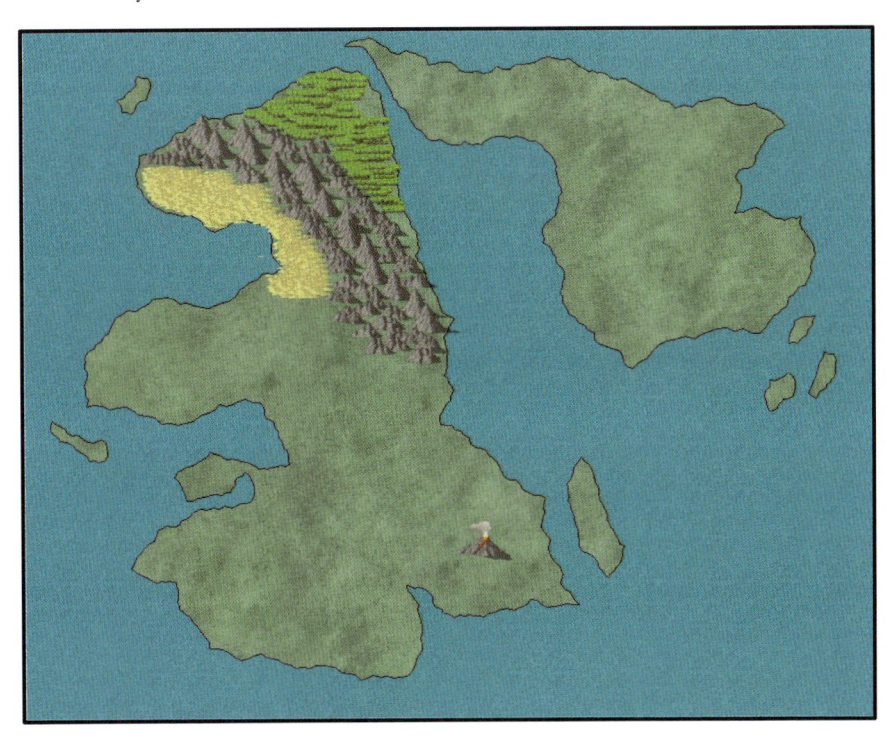

I have now added desert in the rain shadow on the western side of the mountains, and because we know that a lot of rain will fall on the eastern side, I decided to fill the area with jungle terrain. I left a spot open in the farthest northeastern corner, as I imagine that a city will go there – we will place settlements later.

With the creation of fantasy maps there might be a slight tendency to turn it into a checklist: have you got deserts, swamps, forests etc. etc.?

To all intents and purposes this whole book is a form of a tally on its own, but don't worry about it turning cliched. You are mimicking the real world and that is a good thing, but at the same time you don't have to create a perfect mirror of Earth.

I'm conscious that I'm very precise in my approach to fantasy map making, but I would do a bad job in teaching this subject if I did not mention that you shouldn't be concerned about going off-script if you have compelling reasons for doing so. Just know that giving your audience a sense of familiarity creates a much stronger link to *immersion* as they get introduced to your world.

So, just a short status check before we move onto *Step Seven* where we will be looking at islands and lakes. You should know have decided upon the sea, land masses, climate zones, weather patterns, mountains, canyons, faults, deserts and fertile lands for your map.

Not all will necessarily be present on the map, but you will have made a decision one way or another at this stage. In fact, this is a good time to add a short observation: As we add more and more details to the map, I advise you to adopt a less-is-more mindset. There is nothing worse than an overcrowded map.

Alright, if you are ready, let's move onto *Step Seven*.

STEP SEVEN

ISLANDS AND LAKES

ISLANDS

With the basic elements all in place, it's time to add some islands to the map. I love this part because islands add a lot of depth and make the map "come alive".

Islands can form in a variety of ways and the most common reasons are volcanic activity and continental shifts. A well-known real-world example of volcanic-formed islands is the state of Hawaii. It consists of hundreds of islands.

Seafloor volcanoes grow in spurts. During their eruptive phase they can easily add 1,000 feet (300 meters) in size during a few weeks or months. While this is enough to form islands on a shallow seafloor, it's not enough to create one when the average depth of the ocean is 12,000 feet (3,600 meters). Here volcanoes have to go through many growth cycles to eventually breach the sea surface: it's a process that might take hundreds of thousands of years. When they finally do, they are likely to be destined to eventually drown as they subside with the underlying aging seafloor and are worn down by ocean waves.

Continental shifts are the second way in which islands can form, and can happen as either a drift or a collision. In the scenario of a drift, the continental plate breaks apart – it occurs over many hundreds of thousands or millions of years – and creates a string of islands between the land masses. On the other hand, when continental plates collide, they push land up, just like when mountains are created on land, but here it's an underwater mountain that becomes an island.

The third way is by erosion. It can be the strip of land that connects the lower portion of a peninsula to a land mass that erodes and thus turns the peninsula into an island, but it can also happen from deposits of sand. When sand, and other debris, are picked up by water currents and deposited on the same location, it can create islands. The Outer Banks of North Carolina (US) are an example of this:

Source: http://upload.wikimedia.org/wikipedia/commons/6/69/NOAA-_Outer_Banks.jpg All credits to its creators.

In placing islands on your map it's good to know that, because of the underwater volcanic activity, they tend to group together. However, you can also include an isolated, bigger island where the tectonic plates rub against each other. In truth, your options are plentiful, so just look for areas on the map where islands would naturally enhance the overall structure.

Keep in mind that they will all have irregular forms and sizes, so vary the shapes as much as possible.

Speaking of variance: you can also include islands where the volcano is still active and will continue to grow with each subsequent eruption. Such places will be quite fertile and can be made wondrous as well – did anyone say Atlantis?

During *Step Five*, I already included islands on our example map. If you haven't done the same, now is the time to add islands.

LAKES

With islands included, it's time to think about lakes.

Lakes are inland bodies of standing water where the tectonic plates in the Earth's crusts pull apart. This movement creates natural basins that eventually fill up with rainwater. In *Step Five* we talked about fault lines and used San Andreas in California (US) as an example. If you have included a fault on your map, it will often have lakes because of all the tectonic activity.

In most cases, though, lakes were formed as a result of glaciers dating back to the ice age 18,000 years ago. As the thick ice pushed along, it carved into the bedrock (the solid rock beneath the soil) and created crevices. When the ice eventually began to melt, it filled up those basins, and as a result lakes occurred.

Even though there are millions of lakes on Earth, most are located in higher latitudes and in mountainous areas. Canada alone contains almost half of the world's lakes, but you also find Lake Titicaca in the Andes Mountains on the border between Peru and Bolivia. At 1,292 feet (394 meters) below sea level, the Dead Sea is the lowest-placed lake in the world.

I mention these examples in order to show that when it comes to lakes, I find it sensible to use them to imply the general rise and fall of the map and thus keep them near mountains. However, as with the Dead Sea, you shouldn't feel constrained by this. If you want to add a lake in a certain place, go ahead and do so.

Generally speaking, though, lakes will form where a low area is surrounded by higher areas. They will usually have a river that connects it to the sea, as this prevents it from becoming stagnant. If you include lakes within mountains or hills, know that they often form as long, outstretched bodies of water. Since water always runs downhill, a lake frequently appears at the foot of the mountain range, and, just as with islands, create them in as many shapes and sizes as you can come up with. The variation will do your map good.

Here is the example map with lakes added:

I included a lake beneath the mountain range for the reasons explained in this chapter, and in addition decided that the center of the second continent is a lower area than the surrounding lands. Less is more, so don't go overboard in adding lakes to your map.

One or two great lakes are good to have, though. While they are more uncommon in the real world, in a fantasy setting not only are they a unique feature, but also they give opportunity to include a sunken city, or something equally interesting, hidden within the depths. Where the ocean is too dangerous for diving, lakes are the perfect choice.

STEP EIGHT

RIVERS

RIVERS AND HOW TO PLACE THEM

In my opinion, water has a big impact on maps, and it matters a great deal how it is laid out. Rivers not only provide fresh water to the people living around them, but also are the most important land feature because they provide political borders so effectively.

While mountains do the same thing, they tend to totally separate nations, whereas countries on either side of a river can still interact as friendly neighbors, or even deadly rivals.

In adding rivers to your map, you are thus making important decisions about physical landmarks and it will define your continents – just as the Mississippi characterizes North America, and the Nile achieves the same in Africa.

For the majority of fantasy maps, I recommend adding a mega-river for a good reason – if you are mapping an entire world you would obviously need to include many – this is where civilizations will prosper. It's also more than likely that it's along these banks that your world's most ancient cultures would have risen.

Since what is covered here in *Step Eight* will settle political boundaries, fresh water supplies, food for communities, trade routes, and so on, now is also a good time to take a moment and consider what placement of rivers will be most coherent for the setting you are trying to create.

Alright, it's time to get into it...

The path of a river is always determined by the height of the terrain – which is why I left it until now. They flow downward from mountains and will generally head towards the sea.

While that might be obvious, I have seen plenty of maps in my time where the creator didn't understand that water chooses the path of least resistance. If the terrain slopes at 10° to the left, the river will go left, and if there are rocks in the way, it will go around them.

Another common mistake is when rivers leave the mountains, but are then turned to pass through a second mountain range. Because of the extreme elevation involved, it makes for a very unrealistic flow of water.

In fact, rivers won't even cross high regions and instead wander straight towards the sea. Here is a relief map of Southern Italy to serve as a real-life example:

Source:http://upload.wikimedia.org/wikipedia/commons/d/da/Southern_Italy_relief_location_map.jpg All credits to its creators.

Consider your continental divide, or the large mountain range, created during *Step Six,* and use that to decide in which directions your rivers are going to run.

With mountains placed in a north-south configuration, the rivers on the left-hand side will go from the mountains to the sea in the west (including northwest and southwest), while rivers on the right-hand side will head for the sea in the east (including the northeast and southeast).

Similarly, if you decide to have a mountain range crossing the continent from east to west, then the rivers in the lower half will leave the mountains and find the sea on the southern shore. Rivers above the mountain range will continue until they drain into the northernmost seas. In neither case will you ever find rivers flowing from coast to coast.

In places where you included a lake at the foot of the mountains, you will need to make sure that any down-flowing river from the mountain connects to it. Essentially, rivers feed lakes, which in turn drain out at their lowest side to form a new river. Also, because it's the lowest point, there will only be one river leaving a lake, not several.

Thus, make sure to anchor all rivers with a realistic starting point – mountains, hills, or a lake – and once done look to generate some branches. One option is to have sub-rivers flow from several different mountain areas and attach themselves to the mega-river, forging a main stream towards the shore. Alternatively, you can set dozens of major rivers that never get anywhere near the mega-river.

No matter which solution you decide upon, it's important to know, when heading downstream on their continuous path towards the ocean, that rivers will never divide by splitting up, as in one river suddenly becoming two; instead they will combine, as in two rivers joining to become one.

River deltas are also rarer than one might think. They do add a nice degree of variation to the map, though, so if you would like to include some, do so where the water gets close to the coastline. It's a much more realistic place to find river deltas.

Speaking of realism, we all know how the Nile flows through the Sudanese desert, but here I suggest verging on the cautious side. While it's certainly possible to have a river in a desert, it also sticks out to many people as an oddity on a fantasy map. It draws a lot of attention to itself, so there is that *immersion* argument again. I would, unless there is a really good reason for it, decide against such an arrangement.

At the end of the day, since rivers are the main transportation arteries of your world, knowing where they are located will also begin to give you hints as to where to place cities. You can use these natural flows of water to form interesting borders, and if you have a river passing through a narrow valley between two different mountain ranges, such a place would be of extreme strategic importance. On the contrary, a narrow strip of land between two rivers will likely turn into a swamp and make it a very unlikely place to settle. Swamps should, however, only be used with caution. In medieval times they were very hard to traverse and they still are today. Just be careful not to box the characters in too much.

I hope you now see why I mentioned how much I like rivers in the beginning of this chapter. This *Step Eight* spices up the mundane and, at the same time, I often end up getting further ideas. If the same happens to you, make notes of what you want to incorporate as we move through the remainder of this book.

Here is the latest version of our example map:

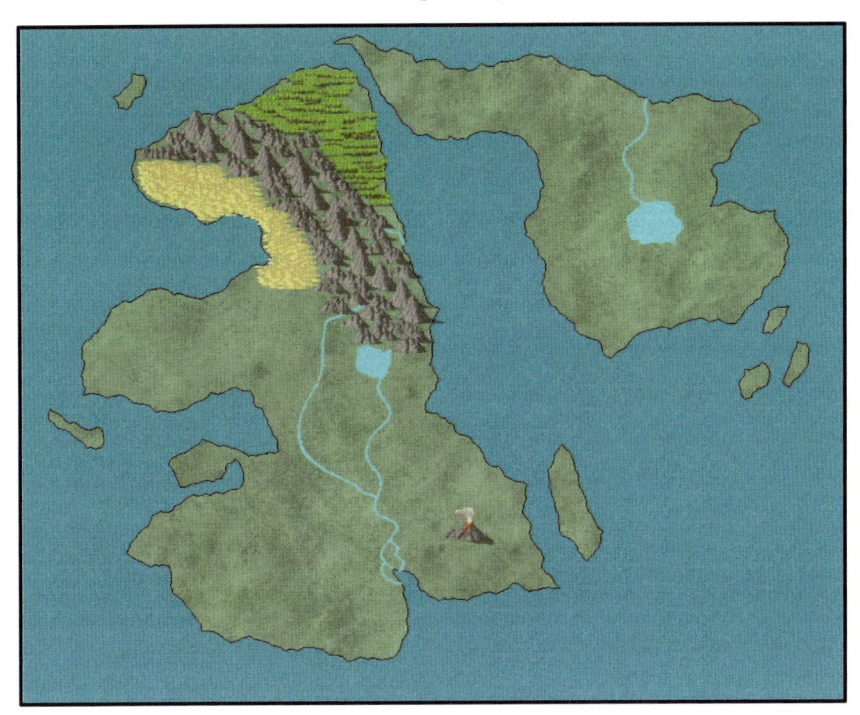

Next, we are going to place forests, but allow me to circle back to glaciers for a brief moment. I talked about these ice giants earlier and should you be interested in creating a winter-themed map, be aware that large rocks would have been pushed away from the polar regions by the growing glaciers and in their wake they will leave behind large holes in which meltwater will fill up. In such a setting, this is what turns into rivers. Over the course of thousands of years, they will continue to erode valleys into steeper and deeper canyons. Waterfalls will not be uncommon either.

STEP NINE

FOREST

AND THERE WERE TREES

I have to say that forests are wonderful enhancements to any fantasy map. Much like rivers and mountains, they can act the part of being natural borders or boundaries, but they also offer hidden areas: places where no one knows what is lurking inside.

However, adding different types of terrain, which varies the look of the map, is as important as using forests. In my opinion, too many world designers end up with maps crammed full of major kingdoms. While that might give a lot of detail about the setting, it offers very little room for exploration. And what is a fantasy world without exciting travels?

Consider the map of *Middle-Earth* which incorporates places like the Dead Marshes, the Gap of Rohan, and the Fangorn Forest. Much of this geography adds depth to the story and the world in which it is set. Therefore, it's my recommendation to fill remaining open spaces on your map with approximately 30% of wilderness. If you go to the end of this book, you will find Appendix B. In that, I have included different types of terrain, or wilderness, for your consideration.

In focusing on forest, the good news is that, for once, there are no rules to take into consideration, other than the fact that forests don't border deserts. Here you will have to use plains or scrublands instead.

Other than that, woods can appear just about anywhere, but they are often in close proximity to mountains because of the presence of water.

Forests come in any shape or form, from dense groupings to small clusters of trees representing a peaceful and quiet spot of seclusion.

A STEP-BY-STEP GUIDE FOR WORLDBUILDERS

With wilderness included in our example map, it's really beginning to take form. No one is living on these lands as of yet, so let's change that and head into *Step Ten*.

STEP TEN

COUNTRIES

NATION-BUILDING

Fantasy stories are often about heroes and the fate of nations.

In this context we can't ignore how a country's culture and history play an integral role. While building cultures do go beyond the scope of this book on map making, and belong in a book on worldbuilding, I still want to scratch the surface of this topic because, at this stage, it interlocks so strongly with the process of map creation.

Consider the different nations that will be featured in your story or setting, and then proceed to understand how the landscape will influence them or vice versa. Maybe you already know that you want a seafaring nation, and their enemies are a secluded people. Hence, you have to create places for each on your map.

What is important is that you either let the outlay of the land affect its people's culture, or you infuse the map with elements that a certain culture would demand. For instance, the Mongols were a steppe people and, for that reason, they were the best horse archers in the world. If you have horse archers make sure that they live in open-space lands, or if you have an open-space country, maybe that is what inspires you to create a nation of horse archers.

You have some leeway, though, because places will change over time! One nation could have a background as a seafaring nation even if you decide not to include any trees to build boats from on their lands.

Spain serves as an excellent example here. They do not have many forests, but during medieval times they were a nation of tremendous naval capability, maybe surpassed only by the British. All the forests in Spain were cut down when Rome and Carthage fought the Punic Wars. They wanted to control the trading routes over the Mediterranean Sea, and to do that, they needed ships. However, in Africa and Italy, forests were scarce, so they took timber from Spain.

Having an understanding of each nation's culture before adding them to the map will inform your worldbuilding, and in addition, it can also tell you something about the political power scale. Bigger countries are more likely to be more dominant and perhaps there are even internal divisions of power within each nation. Weaker nobles might be fighting over control for certain city states, while major players are perhaps the more obvious choice for an epic conflict in your fantasy world.

This is where you can let the natural borders, like mountains, rivers and forests, come into their full right and either inflate or diminish tensions across the political spectrums. Obtaining a basic understanding of your nations, and even considering what kinds of plants and animals will thrive in the climate zone you decided upon in *Step Six*, will all make for a rich and interesting world, whether it's intended for fiction or gaming.

COUNTRIES AND BORDERS

If your map did not already feel alive, it certainly will now that the nations enter the scene.

This is also one of my favorite parts of map making, and as explained earlier, it makes sense to make borders run along natural obstacles. By now, we have familiarized ourselves with how rivers, sea coasts and mountains can form excellent boundaries. But what if there are no natural dividers? What if it's only a political border right at the center of a conflicted steppe?

First of all, pure political borders tend to be rare, but where they do exist, they will be in constant flux and often result in a certain level of tension between the nations on either side.

While peaceful neighbors of course are an option, it's always more interesting when there is a certain agenda in play. Perhaps one nation is using the other to boost their own position, or they are secretly undermining the other's authority. Whatever it is, you are usually better off with conflict and scheming than without.

With all that said, do keep in mind that your nations have to be able to exist. What I mean is: make sure that they have functioning trade routes and at the same time borders that are defendable.

In *Step One*, I mentioned the free worksheet. Here it is once again: https://www.jesperschmidt.com/fantasy-map-making-download/. It will come in handy when it comes to establishing the borders on your map.

A STEP-BY-STEP GUIDE FOR WORLDBUILDERS

I have sketched out where country borders will go on our example map (this information is for your benefit only and should be deleted for the final version of the map):

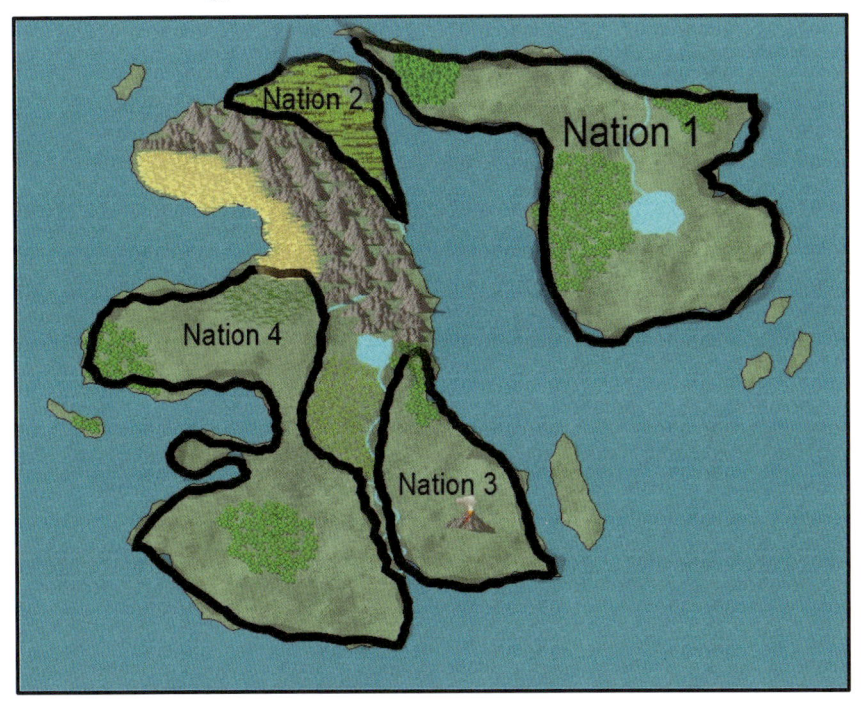

With that completed, look over your map one last time. Are there any areas which look too large and barren? If so, keep dividing this vast, unclaimed territory by political borders until you are happy with it.

Having large regions is only going to get a cursory consideration of the terrain, whereas smaller regions are going to allow for a more realistic mix of features. In other words, a giant mass of land on your map, full of mountains, will most likely be a lot less interesting than three subregions of mountains, forests and hills.

There is nothing wrong with a few bigger areas on the map, though, and it all comes down to scale of course, but settling with too many is only a missed opportunity to make your world better and more interesting. As an example, it might be a good idea to leave some areas beyond the reach of any nations: an untamed, unexplored wilderness where no one knows what they will find.

SETTLEMENTS

As mentioned under *Step Eight*, people tend to settle near water. A population of thousands demands not only a water supply, but also the capability to transport goods and conduct trade. The biggest of cities will be found at the most prominent and strategic spots, being a river, a lake, or by the ocean. Just consider London or Paris.

If you were to place a settlement ten miles from a water source, your audience would likely wonder why the people didn't just move next to the water. So, try not to break *immersion* with small but important mistakes like this.

Let's begin by placing the major population centers, and in doing so, this is the first time that I will ask you to go against reality and actually add an unrealistically low number of settlements when comparing to medieval Europe.

Creating an overcrowded map is not good for a fantasy setting, so I prefer to keep within a range of six to twelve named locations on my world map. It's a rule of thumb that varies depending on the size of your setting, but I honestly don't think you will be doing anyone a favor by creating a map with thirty named cities on it. I recognize this is a matter of taste and personal preference, and I'm just giving you mine.

Once the largest cities have been included, it's time to add some towns. Three to six is usually more than enough, and I recommend skipping villages altogether on continent- or world-scale maps. Such details are better suited to close-ups of individual kingdoms.

Unlike cities, towns don't need to be situated next to water. While it's a realistic choice to settle next to a river branch or a small lake, you have more artistic freedom with these. Just remember that the community has to have a way to support itself.

Scatter towns across the map if you like. The town on the shoreline, between two cities, would probably be midway to allow ships to stop when the weather conditions would demand it. Any town in the middle of nowhere would likely have valuable resources close by, and the town that exists far away from the rest of the realm probably functions as a caravan town. Whatever your choice might be, it strengthens your setting if you can give each one a unique flavor.

Make sure to have a reason in mind when you place settlements on the map. It should never happen at random. If it does, I can almost guarantee you that most people will notice.

Here is our example map, now with people living on it:

Apart from what I have already mentioned – e.g. trade routes, access to mining or water – there are a few other reasons why a city or town might form. It could be on lands suitable for agriculture, or perhaps for religious reasons if a holy site is close by. Or how about an aggressive neighbor causing a formation of cities to act as a defensive parameter?

STEP ELEVEN

ROADS

ARTERIES OF A NATION

We are really getting into the home stretch of the map making process and from here on, it's all about details. The first one is roads: the highways which define your arteries of trade and commerce.

Just like water, main roads tend to follow the path of least resistance. They run along rivers, coastlines, across desolate countryside, or through slender mountain passes. The nature of man is that we prefer to lay a thirty-mile road through rolling hills rather than five miles up a steep mountain. So, for the most part, roads will be relatively straight, and in a fantasy world there shouldn't be too many of them either.

While a true-to-life medieval map would have roads running this way and that way, it's better to let only a few roads run between cities and towns. Too many connections won't make a better map.

Start by connecting capital cities unless there are good reasons not to. If two nations are mortal enemies, it is not likely that anyone would build a road to the front door of the man who wants them dead. You could also have a situation where the nations are so far apart that it wouldn't make any logical sense for a road to have been established.

Once you have the main roads in place, I want you to move onto trade routes. Humans also build roads to connect us to the resources we want. If we know where certain goods, luxury items, or materials are located, we will want to establish trade roads to connect buyer and seller.

A STEP-BY-STEP GUIDE FOR WORLDBUILDERS

This is where Nation-Building, from *Step Ten*, should help to determine which nations would be interested in which type of goods. If this process leads you to two or more roads converging, then place a city there as well. Only a fool wouldn't want to settle in the epicenter of trade.

As a final action, add a few smaller and less traveled roads that connect to any of the smaller cities or perhaps particularly important landmarks. These are just included to give an impression of detail and completeness to the map.

Here is what it looks like:

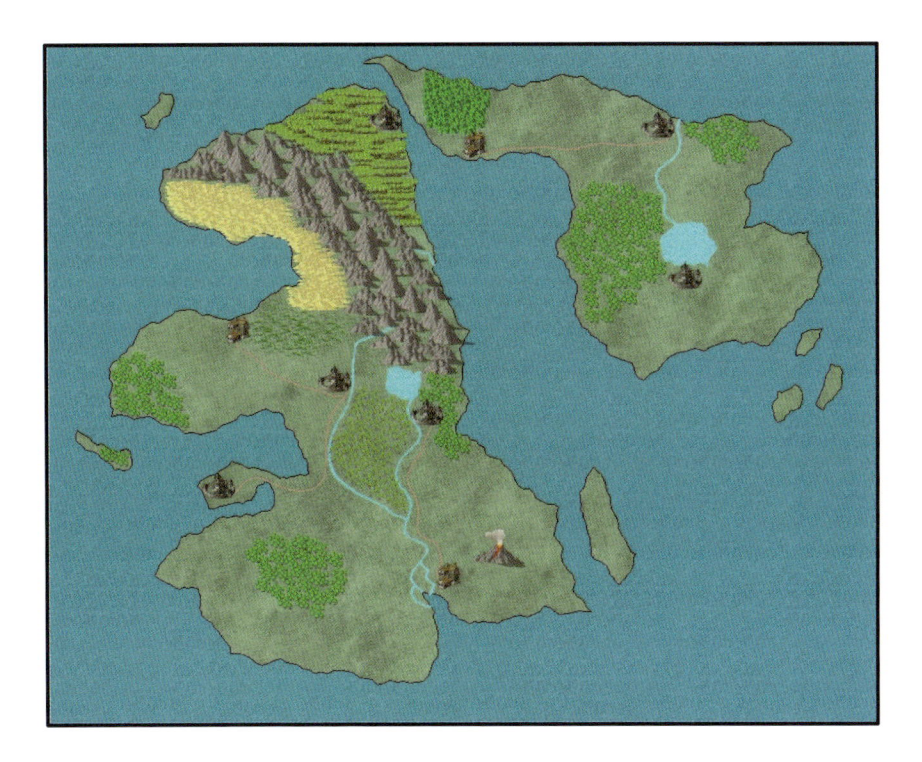

STEP TWELVE

FANTASY

WAIT... WHERE IS THE FANTASY?

So far, I have talked a lot about realism, but we shouldn't forget about fantasy. Where has it all gone?

While this step is a purely optional one – it solely depends on the story and the world you are creating – I do believe that it will be applicable to most of us with every new map.

Before we head into the map key, brainstorm a few truly weird and wondrous locations. They can be places of evil or good: it matters not. It could be an underground lair, a magic portal, an old ruin, a dragon's lair, a ghost town... anything. Perhaps you don't even know what they are, only where they are located. That is all fine as long as no ruler or landowner controls it.

For the most part, these places should be situated away from cities and towns. If they aren't, they would likely have had a lasting effect on the population, which does require a certain level of explanation to your audience.

One or two of these landmarks are usually more than enough, unless your setting is a really crazy one where rivers run up mountains and the water is colored red. You might even find it useful to create something that nations will be fighting over, something they want to control or gain access to. It could also be something that everyone is fighting to get away from.

Essentially there is no limit to how far you can let your imagination take you. Who said a floating city atop a huge, bottomless pit at the center of the world? Go ahead... you can steal the idea...

A STEP-BY-STEP GUIDE FOR WORLDBUILDERS

I have now incorporated a fantastic place to our example map – a giant obelisk on the southern shore – and we are nearing the end:

STEP THIRTEEN

FINAL TOUCHES

THE MAP KEY

Well done. You are now the proud owner of a world with mountains, hills, deserts, jungles, islands, rivers, lakes, bays, woods, countries, roads, and maybe touches of fantasy. Wow, that was a mouthful, and you are almost done.

You can now include the "map key", sometimes referred to as the "map legend".

Some prefer to create the "famous box" which explains how to "read" the map, but you can leave that out. In either case, below are the elements you need for the "map key".

A compass

This is a simply a small drawing, somewhere on the map, which shows the four major directions of north, south, east, and west. It helps the viewer to orientate your world, but a slimmed-down version with nothing but an arrow pointing north is also sufficient.

A scale

A scale is a line, usually on the edges or corners of the map, which shows distance. Most software programs will offer built-in features for this. However, if you decide to draw by hand, I would calculate the scale of the map by measuring the overall size first and then divide the distance the map covers by the inches of your drawing. Let's say that your map covers an area of 1,000 miles and the drawing is 10 inches wide, then your scale would be 1 inch = 100 miles. The scale itself is created by drawing a 1-inch line and marking it as "1 inch = 100 miles", or you can draw it 2 inches long and label it as 200 miles.

Adding depth

This part takes practice and is also one of the reasons that I use a professional. The map will be much more visually appealing when you add texture, e.g. shades of gray on mountains, placing small ripples to show waves in the water, small trees on the edge of forest areas. You can also add parchment curls at the edges of the map itself, or even medieval-style borders.

All of these are purely aesthetic improvements, but they make a huge difference. The options are plenty, but in my experience, most are often easier said than done. If you use software, you will have quite some help in this area, but I don't think it looks nearly as beautiful as a professional cartographer can make it. It's up to you.

Names

I'm a strong believer in names, and any major landmark on your map should feature one. A volcano, a glacier, a church, an ancient ruin, a major fortress, regardless of what it is, it should be named separately. The same applies to your world, too.

Earlier in this book, I compared *The Lord of the Rings* to *A Song of Ice and Fire*, and once again, I find it relevant when it comes to the significance of place names.

The name *Middle-Earth* itself comes from the Old English word, 'middangeard'. Tolkien translated this as "the name for inhabited lands of Men between the seas".

He also explained that he uses this name to indicate that the stories of *The Lord of the Rings* are meant to take place "in a period of the actual Old World of this planet".

Furthermore, the place names are also tied linguistically to the history of *Middle-Earth*. As an example, Gondor was originally populated by Númenóreans (the people of the First Age) who formed an alliance with the Elves. Because Númenóreans spoke Elvish, Gondor is also a form of Elvish.

Another example is the earlier mentioned Minas Tirith, which means "The Tower of Watch" in Elvish.

In Westeros (from George R. R. Martin's, *A Song of Ice and Fire*) places are named, Winterfell and Riverrun, which shows off the seats of the powerful noble families. Much like Tolkien, Martin is heavily influenced by medieval history in that his place names reflect the language and history of the worlds he has created. The names of settlements in Westeros are in English, and will look familiar to those who speak English as their mother tongue. One example is the fortress Barrowton. "Ton" is Old English for estate or homestead.

All of this is not to say that your fantasy names in any way have to be rooted in the real world – not at all. My intention it merely to prove a point. If you have logical reasoning behind your naming convention, it will be much stronger than just adding names at random.

DUE DILIGENCE

It's now time to take a break… No, seriously.

Leave your map alone for a while. Once you return, go back over each of the steps we have covered throughout this book and review your map with a fresh pair of eyes. I can almost guarantee you that such a break will make you spot something to modify. Just keep at it until you are happy with the end result.

STEP FOURTEEN

THE

MAP MASTER

DOCUMENTING THE REALM

This *Step Fourteen* verges on the edge of actual worldbuilding, which is not the remit of this book. However, a fantasy map is a useful tool that can certainly fuel your worldbuilding.

Here and there, throughout the pages of this book, I asked you to make some notes when inspiration hit you. Personally, I prefer to translate such ideas into a written overview, or what I call *the Map Master*.

Below is my template, and all you need to do is fill in the blanks for each nation of your setting. The Map Master is also included in the free worksheet (This was the link: https://www.jesperschmidt.com/fantasy-map-making-download/).

THE MAP MASTER

Country Name: The name you have given the country.

Terrain: Short description of the general lay of the land. What kind of atmosphere do you want to convey to your audience?

Climate: Take inspiration from *Step Six*.

Relationships: A note on the relationships with the other nations of the world.

Power: The might of the country compared to others.

Resources: The amount and types of valuables available to the country.

Population: Include numbers on how many people are living in each of the cities and also in the countryside. If your setting features different races, it's worth mentioning them here, too, with a note on how many of each is common to be found.

Fantastic Places: A description of the weird and wondrous locations added in *Step Twelve*.

Beast, Monster and Wildlife: Details on specific creatures unique to this country.

The *Map Master* will generate new ideas and add details which enhance your worldbuilding. So, use the map as a tool to communicate with your audience about the specificities of your world. When characters are traveling from one place to another, make sure to check your map for inspiration. What types of terrain will they pass over? Are there any important landmarks in close proximity?

It's a source of inspiration, but also a fact-checker. If characters travel to the neighboring city, but it's over two hundred miles away, that is not going to happen overnight.

FINAL WORDS OF IMPORTANCE

There is one question I have seen asked over and over again. But before I tell you what it is, I want to thank you for taking the time to follow my step-by-step process for fantasy map making. It's my hope that you learned something along the way.

For some, the creation of a map can be a daunting task and it has been my mission to make the experience seem simple and manageable. To that end, I hope I have succeeded.

You certainly *do not* have to be a great artist to make an incredibly rich map of your world, yet, a good map is what increases the level of *immersion* with your audience. This leads me to the question I have seen posted so often on social media, and that is: "Do I create the map or the world first?"

By now, it's probably pretty obvious how I think that maps and stories go hand in hand, which also makes the two hard to separate. In my opinion, though, the creation of the map should come fairly early in the process of worldbuilding. A map tends to ground me well into the setting, and from there new concepts and details often emerge.

So, that's it.

I have nothing more to teach you and I hope you will go on to create many more maps in the future. When you do, send me a picture of the result on Twitter: http://twitter.com/SchmidtJesper. I would love to see it and most certainly give you a *Like* in return. Even if the map is a crude one, drawn with the kids' crayons, I still would like to see it.

The world can never have too many fantasy maps in it.

❦

Enjoyed this book? You can make a big difference.

Reviews are the heart and soul for the success of a book. It's by far the most effective way for me to get the attention needed for my books.

If you enjoyed the read and found the instructions helpful, I would be extremely grateful if you could spend just two minutes and leave a review at your preferred retailer. If you prefer to keep it short, that is fine, too.

You can jump directly to the retailer page by clicking this link: http://books2read.com/u/mer7Z4

❦

APPENDICES

APPENDIX A: LIST OF TOOLS

URL links to all the tools mentioned in this book:

Adobe Illustrator – http://www.adobe.com/products/illustrator.html

Campaign Cartographer 3 – http://www.profantasy.com

Fractal Mapper – http://www.nbos.com/products/fractal-mapper

GIMP – http://www.gimp.org/

Inkarnate – http://www.inkarnate.com

Photoshop – http://www.photoshop.com/products

APPENDIX B: TERRAIN SUB-TYPES

Polar Terrain

Avalanche Peaks
Coniferous Forest
Frostlands
Frozen Fields
Frozen Swamps
Frozen Wetlands
Geyser Snowfields
Glacial Flats
Glaciers
Ice Fields
Ice Spires
Ice Caps
Icy Floodlands
Icy Hills
Impassable Peaks
Permafrost Wetlands
Polar Desert
Slippery Ice Tundra
Snow Forest
Snowfields
Taiga
Windswept Barrens

Temperate Terrain

Alps
Backwoods
Badlands
Barren Mountains
Bushlands
Coniferous Forest
Crests
Deserts
Dried Mudflats
Dunes
Farmland
Fields
Flatlands
Floodlands
Forested Hills
Forested Mountains
Forested Plains
Grasslands
Groves
Highlands
Lost Valleys
Lowlands
Meadows
Misty Mountains
Mudflats
Pastures
Plateaus
Prairie
Rain-shadow Hollows
Rocky Summits
Salt Marshes
Scrubland
Slopes
Steppes
Stormy Mountains
Swamps
Thickets
Uplands
Valleys
Wastelands

Wetlands
Wilderness

Tropical Terrain

Barrens
Deserts
Dunes
Farmland
Hilly Jungle
Jungle
Marshland
Mudflats
Quicksand Flats
Rainforest
Savannah
Scrublands
Swampy Forest
Tropical Grassland
Tropical Summits
Volcanic Plains
Volcanoes

MORE BOOKS BY JESPER SCHMIDT

The Keystone Bone trilogy

Desolation, volume 1
Degradation, volume 2
Damnation, volume 3

Non-fiction

How to Write a Fantasy Book Description

Plot Development: A Method for Outlining a Novel

Plot Development Step by Step: Exercises for Planning Your Book

Story Idea

Visit: http://www.jesperschmidt.com/books/

LET'S CONNECT ONLINE

Facebook

Catch up with me on Facebook.

I usually post about my next project and feature videos a couple of times a week. I would love to connect and hear more about you.

What do you enjoy in fantasy? Head on over and let me know.

http://bit.ly/28NJQXO

YouTube

I create new videos every single Monday and if you like fantasy settings, worldbuilding and character creation, then this is the place to be.

The focus of the channel is to inspire each other to become masters at crafting immersing fantasy.

http://bit.ly/1WIwIVC

Twitter

I'm very active on Twitter and if you follow me there I will follow you back.

I love connecting with readers, so don't be shy.

http://bit.ly/28O3ArW

ABOUT THE AUTHOR

I have always loved creating, and I suppose that if I was only allowed to choose two words to describe myself they would be "focused ambition". Yet, the art of writing was something that lived a quiet life, in the back of my mind, for many years. It was a dormant desire and, like so many of our dreams, it was placed on a list of things to do later – you know, when time would allow it. And there I left it. Half-forgotten. For a long time.

I have a Finnish sauna to thank for eventually picking it up from that dusty corner and beginning to pour my focused ambition over it. Every summer my wife, two boys and I go to Finland and spend a couple of weeks trying to do as little as possible. In that cottage it is all about slowing down and recharging our batteries. The atmosphere is perfect for it. What was it exactly that sparked my authorship I cannot say for sure – maybe it was just slowing down that gave another perspective. Maybe I was just ready for it. Whatever it was, I am ever-thankful that it happened when it did back in 2015.

Why wait when you can act today?

Find out more here: http://www.jesperschmidt.com/about

Printed in Great Britain
by Amazon